DEATH
AT THE
MOVIES

DEATH

AT THE

MOVIES

HOLLYWOOD'S GUIDE TO THE HEREAFTER

LYN AND TOM DAVIS GENELLI

QUEST

BOOKS

Theosophical Publishing House
Wheaton, Illinois * Chennai, India

Quest Books
Theosophical Publishing House
PO Box 270
Wheaton, IL 60187-0270

www.questbooks.net

Cover image: X-etra/Shutterstock.com
Cover design by Drew Stevens
Typesetting by Wordstop Technologies, Chennai, India

Library of Congress Cataloging-in-Publication Data

Genelli, Lyn.
Death at the movies: Hollywood's guide to the hereafter /
Lyn and Tom Davis Genelli.
     pages   cm.
Includes index.
ISBN 978-0-8356-0916-6
1. Death in motion pictures. 2. Motion pictures-Religious aspects-Buddhism.
I. Genelli, Tom Davis. II. Title.
PN1995.9.D37G46 2013
791.43'6823-dc23   2013006764

5 4 3 2 1 * 13 14 15 16 17

Printed in the United States of America

To the one light and all its reflections.

Movies are not only not reality, they're also not even about reality.

—Mick LaSalle, *San Francisco Chronicle*

For such creatures of luxury as Americans, dharma Is most digestible between slices of entertainment— like movies.

—Dean Sluyter, *Cinema Nirvana*

It is not how things are in the world that is mystical, but that it exists.

—Ludwig Wittgenstein, *Tracticus Logico-Philosophicus*

CONTENTS

INTRODUCTION

And God said, Let there be light: and there was light.

—Genesis 1:3

Our scenario begins with the advent of the "talkies." Based on a Broadway play, the film *Outward Bound* (1930) set a precedent for realistic depiction of the afterlife, devoid of fleecy clouds and heavenly choirs, suggesting rather that the condition of being dead looks and feels pretty much like our everyday lives and that the immediate problem is how to awaken to our true circumstances before we make our situation even worse.[1] The film implies that life and death are in some way the same and that what we do in one realm is manifest in the other. It provocatively evokes the concept of life as a divinely ordained task for each individual, the notion of suffering as retribution for sins in other lifetimes, the theory of rebirth in higher or lower planes, and the existence of transcendent souls that act out links of destiny with other souls through continuing incarnations on various interacting planes— all in all, a heady amount of metaphysical content to find at the Bijou on a Saturday afternoon in 1930.

The film was remade in 1944 as *Between Two Worlds*, one of many popular afterlife fantasy dramas produced during the World War II years that, consciously intended or not, provided comfort for those at home grieving for loved ones lost to the ravages of war. Taken as a body, these films, so uplifting in their intent were, years later, accorded

1

genre status as "film *blanc*," a counter to the popular post-war film noir genre that explored the dark underbelly of America's social reality.[2] Film blanc included such classics as *Here Comes Mr. Jordan* (1941), *Casablanca* (1942), *A Guy Named Joe* (1943), *Blithe Spirit* (1945), *Angel on My Shoulder* (1946), *A Matter of Life and Death* (released in the United States as *Stairway to Heaven*, 1946), and America's most beloved Christmas movie, Frank Capra's *It's a Wonderful Life* (1946), all released or in production during the war years. When the war ended the country returned to a specious normalcy and film blanc lay dormant as its audience's mood turned to the nation's unacknowledged trauma, reflected in motion pictures by film noir, a genre that explicitly denied all possibilities of transcendence to portray a world of violence, cynicism, and death.

For a number of sociological and historical reasons to be pondered in this book, film blanc was powerfully resuscitated in 1980 with the release of the ironically, but appropriately, titled *Resurrection*, closely followed by (noting only major releases) *Poltergeist* (1982), *Beetlejuice* (1988), *Field of Dreams* (1989), *Ghost* (1990), *Jacob's Ladder* (1990), *Defending Your Life* (1991), *Groundhog Day* (1993), *Heart and Souls* (1993), *Sixth Sense* (1999), *Birth* (2004), and *Hereafter* (2010). In a way the genre had never really run its course, but rather gone underground, its themes encoded into any number of popular ghost and fantasy films of the postwar period—films such as *The Ghost and Mrs. Muir*, *Portrait of Jennie*, or *Heaven Only Knows*.

That a transmuted form of the film-blanc genre would eventually resurface is not surprising given that the subject—death and the transition of the soul from one life to another—has been an abiding theme from the very beginnings of storytelling. The development of culture in human societies has generally involved a view that death is a journey, a release from the limited physical realms of time and space into the unlimited and measureless universe of spirit—infinite, eternal, and transcendent. The classic civilizations of the West—Egyptian, Sumerian, Persian, Greek, Roman—all postulated some type of afterlife, and usually an intermediate period between existences that includes a trial or judgment to determine the direction the soul would take on its eternal journey. In Egypt the departed experienced the trial as a judgment in the Hall of Double Law, where one's heart, emblematic of the conscience, was weighed by the deity Osiris against a feather, emblematic of the law. On the pan of the scale weighing the heart sat a dog-headed ape. Behind the scale was a hideous demon whose function was to eat the unjust dead. In the West, we know the rewrite of this scenario as Judgment Day, with its polarity of heaven and hell.[3] Such scenarios are the mother's milk of philosophy and religion, as well as the subject of speculation, debate, fantasy, art, and, of course, the movies. The metaphysical dynamics of these scenarios, provided by history, *and* the popular motion picture, reveal deep and abiding human concerns about the hereafter and how we get there.

That journey, the curious space between death and what lies beyond, is referred to in this book as *transit,* defined by *The American Heritage Dictionary* as "a transition or change, as to a spiritual existence at death."[4] The endless variations of that journey are manifested in the various forms projected by the individual films explored in this book. Each film exposes a unique variation of that ultimate trip. How popular motion pictures have intuited transit through their visions of death and the afterlife, and how those visions play out their largely unconscious role in the evolution and guidance of human consciousness toward understanding the meaning and purpose of death, is the basic theme of this book. We believe the evidence to view such films as vehicles for the subconscious infusion of perennial mystical/spiritual concepts about death and what follows is too compelling to dismiss or deny. At the very least, the subject deserves deeper investigation at social and psychological, as well as metaphysical, levels. Death is, at one and the same time, the most immediate locked door *and* the ultimate frontier, a staggering paradox that invites the mind to venture beyond thought, searching for a deeper understanding based upon a completely different point of view and level of consciousness.[5]

Out of our respect for the innate wisdom of humanity and in the spirit of offering an entertaining look at a serious subject for film lovers, spiritual seekers, and anyone curious about what follows death, we offer this book. If it in any small way provides wisdom about what lies "beyond," that is a bonus prize indeed.

Chapter One

BETWEEN TWO WORLDS

Fantasy and Beyond

Consciousness is a singular of which the plural is unknown.
There is only one thing, and that which seems to be a plurality
is merely a series of different aspects of this one thing, produced
by a deception.

—Erwin Schrödinger

In his 1978 article "The Film *Blanc*: Suggestions for a Variety of Fantasy," Peter L. Valenti singled out for exposition a selection of motion pictures containing uniquely specific phenomena found in the popular genre of motion pictures called fantasy films. Playing off the broad popularity of the film-noir genre of the 1940s and '50s, he called his selection "film *blanc*," suggesting as a specific genre fantasy scenarios embodying the following characteristics: 1. a mortal's death or lapse into dream; 2. subsequent acquaintance with a kindly representative of the world beyond, most commonly known as heaven; 3. a budding love affair; 4. ultimate transcendence of mortality to escape the spiritual world and return to the mortal world.[1]

Valenti's article acknowledges Siegfried Kracauer's *Theory of Film*[2] for its theoretical treatment of fantasy, noting that the American fantasy film grew in popularity during the 1930s, peaked during the early 1940s, and declined in the late 1940s. Valenti points out that different

5

sorts of fantasy combined with angels, pacts with devils, mysterious reincarnations, and beckoning spirits, and that during this general period American film seems to have been entranced by the idea of negotiating between heaven and earth, moving from the mortal plane to the spiritual.

In defining his selection of films Valenti was, at the very least, describing a subgenre of the American fantasy film, somewhat confined by his four characteristics and restricted time frame. He published his article just two years before the release of *Resurrection* (1980), a film that resuscitated the life of film blanc and reflected the spiritual/consciousness/growth/drug movements of America's 1960s and '70s, opening the screen to a body of film blanc–type movies that are the subject of this book. Expanding upon Valenti's four characteristics, we have chosen the term *transit* as the genre identifier, the better to acknowledge the wealth of Eastern spiritual wisdom, particularly Tibetan Buddhism, that added to our Western culture's understanding of and attitude toward death and the beyond.

The subjects of death, the undead, and the beyond have long been popular staples of cinematic entertainment. The fantasy/horror films *Der Golem* (1915), *The Cabinet of Dr. Caligari* (1920), and *Nosferatu* (1922) were silent classics. With the advent of the talkies, coinciding with the Great Depression, came those megahits of horror, *Frankenstein* (1931), *Dracula* (1931), and their progeny, a flood of films dealing with human-made monsters, mummies, ghouls, zombies, vampires, werewolves, and other physical entities that cannot or will not complete the natural process of dying and/or are kept alive through artificial, magical, divine, or diabolic means. Human consciousness is portrayed as a state of helpless identification with some form of corporeal matter, asleep to any purpose higher than basic survival. Believing that when the body dies annihilation of the self occurs, this consciousness develops a greed for material substance, for flesh and blood. Sensual gratifications, whether in the form of eating human flesh and blood or absorbing another's vital energy, become the only things that produce even momentary feelings of life. This dehumanized identification with the body produces as its ultimate expression a form of negative sex—not to reproduce but to perpetuate itself. Vampires are the archetypal figures of negative sex, draining the vital energy from their victims and promising them eternal life, but only as material beings, possessing neither souls nor wills of their own, unable to exist in the light and all it symbolizes.

In *The Wolf Man* (1941), Lon Chaney, Jr., after receiving a hex from a gypsy/witch/shaman (played by the ever-marvelous Maria Ouspenskaya), suffers the bite of a lycanthrope, or werewolf, a human capable of assuming the form of a wolf. True to legend, at the next full moon, Chaney transforms into a werewolf and uses his animal body, not to create another human, but, out of some mad compulsion, to create from an existing human a lunatic replica of himself. In *White Zombie* (1932) and Val Lewton's classic *I Walked with a Zombie* (1943), we see again consciousness trapped in devitalized bodies, without will, controlled by external forces and compelled to take life in order to maintain its own substance. That master of the macabre Boris Karloff, as the Egyptian prince Im-Ho-Tep, is buried alive for committing sacrilege in *The Mummy* (1932). Accidentally brought to life when an unwitting member of an expedition reads aloud the Scroll of Thoth found with his wrapped remains, Im-Ho-Tep kills anyone standing in his path to finding his reincarnated princess and perpetuating their line.

Of interest here is the correlation between high periods of vampire, zombie, and other undead entities in both movies and television and the socioeconomic conditions accompanying their popularity. As one film commentator observed, the two major events of the year 1929 radically affecting America were the Wall Street crash and the arrival of the talking motion picture. Throughout the 1930s gangster and horror movies dominated the screen—unscrupulous robbers and thieving bloodsuckers. Vampires and zombies provided perfect metaphors, covering as they do Wall Street capitalists and their seemingly mindless victims. The best of today's versions of this dynamic, wrapped up in the cloak of the 1-percent-versus-99-percent scenario, are to be found on television, most pointedly with HBO's *True Blood* and AMC's *The Walking Dead*. Not that it can't be found in motion pictures—George Romero reset the bar for the genre in 1968 with his *Night of the Living Dead*, shattering the conventions of horror and metaphorically paving the way for our current national 1 percent–99 percent dialectic.

Angelic, diabolic, and other personified messenger entities such as Death, Time, or Christmas Past traverse multiple planes of existence and interpenetrating worlds for the sake of some grand or horrible design. Often this fantasy variation projects our inevitable confrontation with death in the most conventional of circumstances. *Death Takes a Holiday* (1934), *Green Pastures* (1937), and *On Borrowed Time* (1939) personify death as a humanlike character, an entity we may attempt to reason with, turn toward our point of view, or even outwit. Death is seen as just another consciousness much like our own, and as such is demystified into something more familiar, less threatening. An angel in the form of Jack Benny visits Earth in order to utilize his weapon of mass destruction, Gabriel's trumpet, in *The Horn Blows at Midnight* (1945); another, in the form of Cary Grant, comes to restore Bishop David Niven's faith in *The Bishop's Wife* (1947). And then there is Clarence, angel second class, from *It's a Wonderful Life* (1946), possibly filmdom's best-known and most beloved angelic visitor. Playing from the dark side, we have Walter Huston's perfidious Scratch in *The Devil and Daniel Webster* (1941) and Claude Rains's delightfully malicious Nick, otherwise known as Mephistopheles, in *Angel on My Shoulder* (1946).

Ghosts, another popular variation of the fantasy genre, are spiritual entities that, because of a curse or some unfinished business, are condemned to or choose to maintain their existence on the earthly plane in order to seek redemption or salvation in the resolution of some problematic condition or situation. Trapped in the same existential setting until they awaken to what must be done to break a seemingly perpetual pattern, they cannot complete the process of dying and move on to rebirth in a different situation. Consciousness, instead of being attached to the body, is here attached to the feelings and ideas by which it, when in a physical body, had identified itself as a personality; or it is attached to the people and place it was most comfortable with or to the rectification of some evil deed. Classic examples are a family patriarch's return from the dead to rectify deeds that could cause his daughter suffering in *The Return of Peter Grimm* (1935); Cary Grant and Constance Bennett's unfinished need to help a friend in *Topper* (1937); Veronica Lake's dominating attachment to gaining revenge for perceived wrongs in *I Married a Witch* (1942); Charles Laughton's undying shame about acts of cowardice in *The Canterville Ghost* (1944); a woman's need to reveal vital family secrets to descendants so she can peacefully move on in *The Uninvited* (1944); a dead wife's mischievous desire to hang around to interfere with her living husband's new married life in *Blithe Spirit* (1945); Rex Harrison's realization that even if dead he can provide guidance to another in *The Ghost and Mrs. Muir* (1947); and Jennifer Jones's desire to fulfill her need to be loved in *Portrait of Jennie* (1948).

Ghosts loved to populate the always-welcome subgenre of haunted-house movies. Same situation, a ghosts or ghosts trapped and unable to move on, but now comfortably ensconced in a rundown, dark, and creaky residence. James Whale, director of *Frankenstein* (1931), set the standard for the sound-picture archetype of the haunted-house movie with *The Old Dark House* (1932). With the sterling cast of Boris Karloff, Melvyn Douglas, Charles Laughton, Raymond Massey, and Ernest Thesiger, Whale launched a wave of movies utilizing the haunted-house theme, sometimes for thrills and chills, but often for laughs, like the enormously popular Bob Hope–Paulette Goddard vehicle *The Cat and the Canary* (1939). The film was remade, again with Hope and Goddard, as *The Ghost Breakers* (1940), and yet again as *Scared Stiff* (1953) with Dean Martin and Jerry Lewis at the helm (and there were literally dozens of haunted-house movies in between each of the above). By the 1980s property values on haunted houses had risen to such heights that we were treated to *Ghost Busters* (1984), the first multimillion-dollar scare comedy about removing ghosts from potentially high-valued properties in a major American city.

Judging by the vast, ongoing proliferation of films about demons and demonic possession, this category might accurately be described as the most fruitful of the various fantasy genres, showing consciousness fascinated by the demonic projections of its own repressed sexual and aggressive feelings. Something in the ostensibly pragmatic American character seems more than fascinated, perhaps obsessed, by the possibilities inherent in being possessed or dominated by such forces—perhaps a form of denial of responsibility for exercising our darker desires and fantasies. Here human consciousness can lose faith and abandon or deny its spiritual will. Feeling controlled by forces outside itself, it uses those feelings of possession or domination as an excuse to act out projections that are too cruel, too lustful, too hopeless, or too heinous for the mind to accept as its own. The early classics here are *The Cabinet of Dr. Caligari* (1920), *The Devil and Daniel Webster* (1941), and Val Lewton's *The Seventh Victim* (1943). Progeny of this category, such as *The Devil's Advocate* (1997), seem to dominate the screen today, as though malevolent forces external to ourselves have proliferated to keep pace with ever-growing levels of narcissistic greed and neurotic anxiety.

Rounding out this brief review of the early fantasy/undead genre, we offer the category of those most topically appealing, emotionally dynamic, and humanly relevant movies that address the deepest mystery conceivable, the universal and inevitable journey of human consciousness from one state of existence to the next—the beyond. In the following chapters we will use material grounded in both Western and Eastern religious and philosophical/spiritual teachings to examine some of the motion pictures, from *Outward Bound* (1930) to *Hereafter* (2010), that address issues of life and death common to all human beings. We find these films, beyond conveying ideas rooted in the deepest perennial wisdom of our planet's various cultures and beyond being sometimes funny, sometimes poignant and often uplifting, to be simultaneously enlightening and just plain entertaining.

Chapter Two

FILM BLANC OR TRANSIT

Life is pleasant. Death is peaceful. It's the transition that's troublesome.

—Isaac Asimov

Hollywood's earliest and most charming and curious explorations into the "beyond" were those films dealing with that twilight zone of time and space in which the human spirit, just departed from its body, seeks its place in some cosmically ordained scenario of existence. Such scenarios, showing contemporary humans "successfully negotiating a return to the real mortal world after a trip to the twilight region between life in the physical world and either death or an altered state of existence in another, spiritual world," were described in Peter L. Valenti's seminal 1978 essay, "The Film *Blanc*: Suggestions for a Variety of Fantasy, 1940–45."[1]

Just as the better-known genre film noir depicts the dark, cynical underside of human motivation, oriented toward death, film blanc portrays the upside of human nature, our profound attraction to the spiritually transcendent, to the luminous. Among the films Valenti cites are *Beyond Tomorrow* (1940), *Here Comes Mr. Jordan* (1941), *Between Two Worlds* (1944), *The Horn Blows at Midnight* (1945), and *A Matter of Life and Death* (1946)—seen in America as *Stairway to Heaven*. For Valenti, the importance of these films is historical. They represented the public's (and therefore Hollywood's) need to accept the war-caused deaths of so many loved ones and the desire to be assured that some essential aspect of the person could survive physical death. He points out that these films, while heavily moralistic and sentimental, were mainly of humanitarian value, helping to pacify a public grief. However, humankind's deeper concern about what happens after death is timeless and universal, and film blanc has continued to exist outside the World War II time frame. Every culture posits a myth of transition from death to rebirth on either a higher (heavenly) or a lower (hellish) plane. Since Hollywood movies inevitably reflect humanity's concerns, one can expand upon Valenti's thesis to find a more contemporary and universal significance for the film blanc.

Of the above-mentioned films, *Between Two Worlds* is most literally about journeying in that twilight region between life, death, and beyond, a condition of passage or state of mind that Tibetan Buddhism refers to as the *bardo* and that we refer to as *transit*, as in "transition" or "transitory."[2] A random gathering of people, waiting to board a ship from London to America is hit by a German bombing raid and subsequently experiences a journey to another world. At first, the passengers of the mist-shrouded vessel do not realize they have died. Trying to manipulate reality as they always have, they gradually begin to comprehend their actual situation, despite their various attempts to deny, forestall, or avoid their destiny. Eventually each of them is seen by a kind of judge (Sidney Greenstreet), who assigns to each the particular existence that affords true justice and the opportunity to redeem his or her past mistakes.

The charmingly sentimental comedy *Here Comes Mr. Jordan* portrays a crucial transit-related theme: that an individual has a particular destiny to be fulfilled in a given life, and until that is fulfilled the individual consciousness cannot complete its natural cycle of life-death-transit-rebirth and move on with its development. A prizefighter (Robert Montgomery) crashes his private plane and is taken to heaven, where it becomes clear that a cosmic error has occurred; he was destined to survive, win the championship, and live another forty years. Through an intercession of the heavenly bureaucrat Mr. Jordan (Claude Rains), the prizefighter arranges a return to his body, but finds that it has been cremated; he is offered instead the body of a recently murdered millionaire. Following a traditional Buddhist precept, "Work with what you have," he trains his new self to win the championship. His all-too-human self also proceeds to fall deeply in love. After winning the championship that was destined to be his, the prizefighter is informed by Mr. Jordan that he will now totally fuse with his new identity and remember nothing of the recent celestial error and its subsequent rectification. He is panic stricken that he will no longer recognize the woman he loves (Evelyn Keyes). Minutes later, his consciousness erases of all that has just passed, the lovers meet, and their mutual recognition is achieved instantly through their eyes—the windows of the soul. The film plays lightly and charmingly on the idea that part of what happens in transit is the completion of the previous life's unfinished business. The departed is helped to go on to rebirth and the recognition of the soul's, or self's, true nature, which continues independently, body after body. Its most-reassuring message is that everyone's destiny must be fulfilled and that the cosmic game is fair and trustworthy, even when life seems not to be. At its culminating moment, the film asserts that we are immortal beings passing through different bodies, so that we may eventually arrive full circle, look into each other's eyes, and recognize our eternally journeying selves.

The Horn Blows at Midnight and *Blithe Spirit*, dealing respectively with an angel's visit to Earth to blow Gabriel's mighty horn and thus eliminate a very troublesome planet, and with a ghost whose jealousy won't allow her to move on so her husband can remarry, as well as *A Matter of Life and Death, Angel on My Shoulder*, and *It's a Wonderful Life* were in production or released during the last days of World War II or shortly thereafter. The cessation of hostilities and the painful return to a normal way of life seemed to call for some philosophical conjecture upon the meaning and effects of recent events. These films would seem to point to some collective airing of comforting concepts designed to relieve the sense of loss and futility surrounding the deaths of so many near and dear. However, the deeper question is whether they were merely a mass-produced opiate or whether they point to an innate sense in human beings that life and death are ultimately just and that death is not final.

In Michael Powell and Emeric Pressburger's *A Matter of Life and Death*, a downed pilot, a Royal Air Force Flight Commander(David Niven), returns to Earth after persuading a heavenly official that he should be allowed to live. This supernatural element is rendered admissible by the conceit of making Niven the victim of brain damage acquired in his airplane's crash, causing him to fantasize that his life is in the balance between this world and the next. A neuropsychiatrist (Roger Livesey) implies that the pilot, feeling guilt as the sole survivor of his bomber's crash, is himself unsure whether he deserves to live. He must somehow justify his existence in the light of his comrades' deaths. His fantasy takes the form of a heavenly trial presided over by the wisest men in history on a set magically creating a celestial courtroom, an amphitheater of infinite proportions, most fitting for arriving at what is cosmically ordained. The tone of his trial and the quality of the individuals who preside over it substantiate Valenti's supposition that "perhaps the obvious benevolence of the omnipotent spirits and the kindly character actors who portray them suggest that even when times are difficult and one sees the world crashing about one's ears, there are indeed powers above who will provide and who have ordained these seemingly tragic events for the best."[3] *A Matter of Life and Death* reflected the needs of those at home to be assured that the deaths of their loved ones had been worthwhile and that a benevolent force now watched over their departed in a place of eternal beauty and tranquility. Niven returns to life and to the arms of his lovely nurse (Kim Hunter). Thousands of others did not, but the film provided a lavish and comforting fantasy about that alternative.

Angel on My Shoulder, in which the devil promises leniency to a dead gangster if he will return to Earth and take over the body of a judge who is stamping out evil, is a sort of *Here Comes Mr. Jordan* played from the bottom up. Gangster Eddie Kagel (Paul Muni) is bumped off by Smiley, a trusted partner, and goes straight to hell. Where else? Eddie is a natural denizen of the underworld, having never known anything but crime. He has yet to see a joint he can't crash out of, and hell is no exception. He immediately turns his new abode into a, well, living hell for the trustees whose job is to torment the inmates. This activity brings him to the attention of Nick, otherwise known as Mephistopheles (Claude Rains). Nick is quick to notice Eddie's uncanny resemblance to one Frederick Parker, an incorruptible and humane judge who is running for governor back on Earth. Nick blames Parker for the current labor shortage in hell and sees in Kagel a way to destroy him. He cuts a deal with Eddie, giving him a chance to get even with Smiley in exchange for inhabiting the body of Judge Parker.

Once Eddie assumes the body of the judge nothing goes as planned. Eddie is immediately attracted, in a crude physical way, to Barbara (Anne Baxter), the judge's fiancée, who attributes the judge's unusual behavior to the strain of his political campaign. A psychiatrist friend suggests that she should be patient and do anything she can to help him. At a campaign speech the next day, Eddie, following Nick's plan, is supposed to play the judge as an incompetent rascal, alienating his constituency. But the judge's enemies, thugs hired by his corrupt opponent, arrive at the start of his speech and begin to throw rotten fruit. Instead of politely retreating, as the real Judge Parker might do, Eddie hurls himself from the stage into the midst of the gang and creates a major donnybrook. He is hailed by the press as a hero and seen as a person who will fight to get things done. To Nick's chagrin, every action Eddie takes to discredit the judge has positive results; he becomes the recipient of genuine admiration from the public and a deepening sense of respect and love from Barbara. And for the first time Eddie begins to feel the effect of receiving love and approval. It is a shattering experience, the opening of a whole new world, to feel a warm, glowing sensation he has never felt, to be reborn. He is a bundle of conflicting emotions, and his attraction to Barbara becomes tender and caring. He wants all the things he believes a good life provides—a wife, a home, and children.

His transformation from an instinct-driven, animal-like creature to a loving human being is a strange and difficult territory, and in his confusion he pressures Barbara to marry him. She is torn but recalls the psychiatrist's advice, "Try and help him in any way you can." They find a church and enter the rectory. As they do, Eddie overhears the rector rehearsing his next sermon: "The devil wields no power over a good man. If thy hand offends thee, cut it off. It is better to enter life maimed than to go into the Gehenna of an inextinguishable fire." The words serve to snap Eddie back to knowing what he must do. He tells Barbara, "I can't marry you. I'd be doing wrong. And that's just what the devil's waiting for. My eyes have been opened . . . which don't mean that you lost Fred Parker. You'll be finding him again. And you'll be proud of him." While she doesn't completely understand him, her love makes room for her to accept his words and trust his promise.

Eddie returns home with the intent of leaving Judge Parker's body to resume the course of the judge's life. But when he arrives, he finds Smiley, who has come to bribe the judge so that he can expand his crooked business. Eddie has his promised confrontation with Smiley, but he can't kill him because he no longer feels hatred or lust for revenge. Smiley is somewhat thrown that the person in front of him looks like Eddie, but he manages to say to the judge, "My name's Smiley." The hardboiled Eddie responds icily, "They call me Judge Parker. But maybe I ain't Judge Parker. Maybe I'm somebody else. Someone you know. Maybe I'm that pal of yours, Eddie, Eddie Kagel. The one you chopped down with his own rod."

Smiley completely panics and, overwhelmed by fear, backs away from Eddie in horror and falls out of an open window to his death. Eddie moves quickly to complete what he must do. He makes his peace with Barbara, knowing she will have a good life with the judge. Nick is forced to concede defeat. Eddie withdraws his soul from the judge's body and he and Nick head back to hell.

Walking to the sidewalk elevator that will take them to hell, an irritated Nick says, "When I get you down below I'm going to take special pains with you. I'm going to introduce you to agonies undreamed of." Eddie replies like the true denizen of the underworld he is, "Ahhh! I don't think you'll be so tough. 'Cause you know why? 'Cause you made a sap of yourself. You don't want your boys to know that. No big shot wants to look like a sucker before his whole mob. Now, if I was made a trustee . . . " As they descend into the smoky depths, Nick answers with pretended indignation, "Why this is sheer, unblushing blackmail."

And as they disappear we hear Eddie's final words: "You oughta know brother, you oughta know."

While entertaining and appealing, *Angel on My Shoulder* mostly avoids the essence of the transit experience, conveying rather the sentimentality and pop mysticism of its fanciful plot. Like most film blanc, it manages to sidestep the issue of death in favor of a more sympathetic treatment of the living—a not-unworthy policy, and certainly one appropriate for the times, as well as safer at the box office. The critic Andrew Sarris wisely observed that this failure to deal with the real issue was duplicated by the reigning critics of the day, who preferred to focus on the aesthetic quality of the fantasy rather than on the issue of death itself.[4] More to the point, in retrospect, was their inability to confront those aspects of transit that are most relevant to the living: the basic metaphor of psychological transformation inherent in the subject of death and its consequences. This confrontation would be fully achieved in Frank Capra's *It's a Wonderful Life.*

Chapter Three

THE LIGHT AND DARK SIDES OF OUR SITUATION

It's a Wonderful Life and Dead of Night

The situation in which we find ourselves is only the secondary cause of our suffering. The primary cause is our innate ignorance and the resulting desire for things to be other than they are.

—Tenzin Wangyal Rinpoche

That our "desire for things to be other than they are" is a major cause of universal unhappiness seems pretty obvious. But what exactly is this "innate ignorance" that is claimed to be the primary cause of our cravings? In Buddhist practice the term *innate ignorance* is central to the concept of consciousness of self. It is, in essence, a deep misperception of reality and of reality's fundamental nature as *emptiness*,[1] meaning that nothing possesses any essential, enduring identity because all things are relative, conventional, contingent, or interdependent— without separate existence of their own. Innate ignorance, being blind to this misperception, functions somewhat like various defense mechanisms, skewing how we view reality to protect our ever-vigilant and oversensitive ego from insult or injury. But it goes deeper than this; for Buddhists, innate ignorance is *the* primary cause of human suffering, going to the very root of how mind generates our sense of alienation, discontent, and fear of death. Eliminating the condition of innate ignorance, the misperception of reality, allows the arising of a state of awareness of, or, better, a state of calm abiding in, the deepest nature of mind. The Buddhist forest monk Achaan Chah, discussing the nature of suffering, points out that there are two forms of suffering, the suffering that leads to more suffering and the suffering that leads to the end of suffering. If one is not willing to face the second kind of suffering, one will inevitably experience the first.[2]

Which takes us to *It's a Wonderful Life* (1946). Director Frank Capra had just completed fourteen films over a four-year period with the US War Department. His last commercial film, *Meet John Doe* (1941), was atypical of him in its darkened, almost hopeless view of the American character and can be seen as indicative of the general paranoia and anxiety immediately preceding America's entry into World War II.[3] *It's a Wonderful Life* marked not only Capra's return to commercial filmmaking after four years of death and destruction, but also his attempt to recapture that magical capacity to affirm consistently his public's belief in the common man. George Bailey (Jimmy Stewart) *is* that common man, come to the end of his faith in living. His greatest wish has always been to "shake the dust of this crummy town off my feet." But destiny has decreed that George spend his life sacrificing his own wishes to the needs of others. He saves his brother's life, only to see his brother go on to lead the life he had imagined for himself. He takes over and rescues his father's business of providing a savings and loan for the little people. He never leaves town, never goes to college, can't go to war, and can't even go off on his own honeymoon trip. Finally, on a snowy Christmas Eve, driven to the edge by the loss of everything he owns, George Bailey contemplates suicide. All hope gone, spiritually a dead man walking, he is poised to jump into the icy waters of the town's river. In that moment, George enters the transit state, transported out of time and space through the grace of his own good works, personified in the presence of his guardian angel. Clarence (Henry Travers), an elderly and affable, if not altogether competent, angel second class, has been sent from heaven to earn his wings by saving the soul of a deserving man. It is no accident that what George's psyche conjures up for his transit guide is yet another being in need. Clarence's most immediate need is to be rescued from the chill waters into which he leaped an instant before George could jump. George, sacrificing even his own suicide to the need of another being, dives into the freezing river to rescue Clarence. In the sobriety of drying off in the bridge-tender's shack George remembers his intent to kill himself. Overwhelmed by his sense of failure, he angrily proclaims the wish that he had never been born, unconsciously setting the terms of his own transit vision. George's wish gives Clarence, who as an angel possesses divine power, tacit permission to reconstruct reality so that it can appear without any trace of George himself.

What follows is "nightmarish and terrifying. Bailey has been saved, but his ordeal has just begun. To be purged of his suicidal wishes, the character is temporarily robbed of all identity, so that even his nearest and dearest fail to know him. It is a powerful fantasy, not to be recognized by your own mother, to find out that your wife never married, became a lonely spinster; to stumble on the grave of the brother whose life you saved, never to have lived!"[4]

George is moved by his experience to an enlightened realization that his life is not only meaningful but that it is the embodiment of perfection itself. He is brought to this realization not by concern for himself (which has never moved him anywhere) but by his concern for others, by the recognition that their lives have been fulfilled because of his presence. George's innate ignorance lay in projecting that his life was a failure rather than part of the perfection that is the essence of reality. The monsters of his transit were those very people who had always needed him, who, unbeknownst to him, had always been his ticket out of town on a one-way trip to heaven. The intensity of his vision brings that truth home and snaps him back to real time at the snowy edge of a small town on Christmas Eve, a time for rebirth. George is reunited with his family and many friends, who only moments before had been the demons of his transit vision, and the divine revelation of his experience is confirmed when his youngest child hears a bell ringing on the Christmas tree: "Listen, Daddy, every time a bell rings an angel gets its wings." Clarence, George's enlightened essential nature, has indeed won his wings.

Capra's film exquisitely makes the point that the difference between heaven and hell is not the *kinds* of experiences you have, but the *quality of your response* to those experiences. George's entry into the transit state, where the essential self can realize how it has constructed the whole life experience that the ego-self keeps resisting, leads him to the recognition and acceptance of his place in the cosmic order. George, of course, has earned his own equivalent of wings in having chosen, throughout his life, the path of suffering that leads to the end of suffering. With this recognition, George is reborn, not into a new infant body, but into the same old George Bailey body and the same old George Bailey life, now transformed, through acceptance, from a hell to a heaven. The film deals powerfully with the transformational qualities inherent in the transit experience. While tinged with darkness, *It's a Wonderful Life* struggles through the dichotomies of hope and despair to ultimate faith in the purpose of life.

Dealing just as directly with transit, but without the glimmer of such faith, was the British chiller *Dead of Night* (1945), a collection of five tales told within the course of an evening to a visiting stranger. The stranger, an architect (Mervyn Jones), elicits these tales from his fellow guests at a country cottage after revealing that he has been caught up in a recurring dream during which each of them tells him a story about a supernatural experience. He finds this dream disturbing because he is unable to remember how it ends; he knows only that it ends in something unspeakably horrible and that he murders a perfectly innocent man. Each guest, in turn, attempts to relieve the architect of his apprehension by telling him a story about his or her own particular brush with the extraordinary. The mode of each story varies, running from bizarre to sinister to chilling to puckish to viciously insane. It is the framing story, however, that of the dreaming architect, that makes *Dead of Night* so delightfully diabolical and more than just another skillful omnibus film such as *Flesh and Fantasy* (1943) or *Twilight Zone* (1983).

As the film begins, we see the architect driving up to an English country home. While still outside its gates, he stops to do a double take on the house, his first sense of déjà vu. As he enters and meets the various guests, he recognizes each as a character in his dream. One of the guests, a psychiatrist (Frederick Valk), attempts to rationalize away the architect's fantasy, but the others (his fellow dreamers) reinforce it with the telling of their own tales. The psychiatrist finally relents, admitting that he too has witnessed a most sensational occurrence, and proceeds to relate the case history of a ventriloquist who was dominated by and finally absorbed into the persona of his dummy. The telling of this final tale precipitates a rapid series of events leading up to the "unspeakably horrible" end of the architect's dream in which he strangles the psychiatrist, a "perfectly innocent man." The architect wakens from his dream to a phone call from a new client inviting him down to the country to discuss a remodeling job. The last shot shows him driving up to the same English country house as at the beginning of the film.

Dead of Night is about a man eternally caught up in transit. The architect's innate ignorance is that he refuses to recognize, and therefore accept, his own projections. He has chosen the suffering that leads to more suffering. What is refused is repressed into the unconscious, and whatever lives in the unconscious is projected out into the world. The psychiatrist, representing the architect's own rational self, repeatedly attempts to inform the dreamer that his dream is not supernatural, that it is a product of his own mind. He even illustrates his point with a story about a ventriloquist whose mind engulfs him altogether. The architect, with the support of the other guests (society), wants to believe that the problem is outside himself, wants to project his fear and anxiety onto some cause other than his own unwillingness to examine his beliefs. So he strangles the psychiatrist, destroying his own rational self, and begins his dream all over again. His innate ignorance forces him into the choice of reliving the horror of uncertainty rather than exposing whatever truth there is to know about himself—that which he believes is unspeakably horrible. Since he cannot make the recognition of self necessary to free him from his dream, he is condemned to repeat the same experiences, the same mistakes, eternally—not an uncommon interpretation of hell and certainly the perfect description of a transit experience that has degenerated beyond the possibility of a favorable outcome.[5]

Throughout the 1940s, films about the afterdeath experience held a powerful emotional impact, though often overlaid with sentimentality. What they told us was that beyond death exists another world, or worlds, in many ways similar to our own. The films imply, though never explicitly state, that all these worlds are projections of mind; this fact is often suggested indirectly by references to the dream state, a blow to the head, or a brush with death. They tell us that consciousness survives death and undergoes a journey or transition from death to rebirth. This transition apparently involves the unraveling of all the previous life's experiences into their essential, archetypal components; the person in transit is in some powerful way confronted with the consequences of his or her life. In a successful transit, the being can recognize and accept these consequences and the eternal self that created them. With that recognition, the being's essential life crisis is resolved, and he or she is reborn into the same circumstances just left, but with a transformed understanding. The implication is that the key to transit, and hence to life and death, is not the ability to manipulate external circumstances, but the grace to recognize manifestations of the eternal self in everything one sees, hears, thinks, does, and *is*.

The film-blanc genre, while producing mostly lighthearted fantasies, conveyed significant and lasting concepts about the possibilities that lie beyond death. These films showed us realms only subtly different from ordinary life, perhaps a bit more prototypical, but still very like the world we know. They implied that consciousness survives death intact and that after death there is some sort of learning journey through which a person completes the unfinished business of the last lifetime and hopefully comes to a state of loving comprehension, thence to be reborn and again forget the transit experience. They told us that after death there is some sort of reckoning, that there are not so much simplistic heavens and hells, but that our lives are the result of our own actions and attitudes, whether we recognize those facts or not. But, most importantly, they consistently suggested that the recognition of those facts, leading to our taking full responsibility for "the situation in which we find ourselves," is the key to opening a process of lifting the veils of "innate ignorance."

Film blanc did all of this, of course, within the context of the theological parameters of that period's Judeo-Christian culture. The essence of the content may have been perennial, but the iconography was definitely mythological, right up to heavenly choirs, billowing clouds, and trumpet-blowing angels or, alternatively, down to smoke-darkened caverns of hellfire, brimstone, and sadistically amusing devils.[6] *The Catechism of the Catholic Church*, the official exposition of the church's teachings, speaks of the "cleansing fire." It quotes the expression used by Pope Gregory the Great (AD 540–604), *purgatorius ignis* (purifying fire), to explain the church's doctrine regarding the dead's chance of gaining atonement for their sins in order to avoid the eternal fires of hell.[7] It prescribes purgatory as the necessary purification from "an unhealthy attachment to creatures," a purification that "frees one from what is called the 'temporal punishment' of sin," a punishment that "must not be conceived of as a kind of vengeance inflicted by God from without, but as following from the very nature of sin."[8] Or, we would state, the very nature of the cosmos: as ye sow, so shall ye reap. This purification process is fair! As anyone who has really done so will tell you, taking genuine responsibility for our thoughts and deeds, seeing through our ego-protecting defenses, can certainly seem like an eternity in a very painful place. It took until 1999 for Pope John Paul II to issue an official declaration that the term *purgatory* does not indicate a physical place, but "a condition of existence."[9]

Removing the notion that purgatory was a physical realm of corporeal suffering was a return to ancient pre-Christian wisdom-school teachings that pain endured as atonement for one's transgressions must be an act of voluntary, conscious suffering, that is, suffering accepted, neither resisted nor projected outward. This intentional act could create within oneself a metaphorical crucible, a fiery internal furnace, burning away the dross impurities of the soul. One gradually turns from the attachments and mistaken identifications of one's former life toward the Divine. Earthly love is love of a subject for its object. It reflects the inherent separation perceived by the thinking mind and the senses. Heavenly love is the love of Being for itself, that which is one with everything—no duality of subject and object. In purgatory earthly love becomes heavenly love. The film blanc often illustrated this process. In *Angel on My Shoulder*, even in the depths of hell Eddie Kagel can wring redemption out of the devil.

Chapter Four

A MORE INFORMED VISION?

Resurrection

If we could just love each other, as much as we say we love Him,
I 'spect there wouldn't be the bother in the world there is.

—Grandma Pearl, *Resurrection*

The almost-total absence of transit themes in motion pictures during the 1950s and 1960s prompted critic Andrew Sarris to wonder if the enormous commercial success of Warren Beatty and Buck Henry's *Heaven Can Wait* (1978) might not revive the long-dormant afterlife-fantasy genre so popular in the 1930s and 1940s.[1] In actuality, for all its efforts to be contemporary, Beatty and Henry's remake of *Here Comes Mr. Jordan* remained frozen in 1941. Their charming, but literal, Technicolor reproduction added little to the development of popular ideas about the afterlife. As it turns out, any number of cultural and social factors contributed to the revival and enrichment of the transit genre. Primary were the consciousness, growth, and drug movements of America in the 1960s and 1970s.

The wholesale ingestion of a veritable feast of Eastern spirituality during this period initiated large segments of Western society into a far-broader comprehension of ancient concepts of death and transcendence. China's 1949–51 invasion of Tibet launched a major diaspora of the Tibetian culture's teachers and teachings into both Europe and the United States, manifesting in the founding and flowering of numerous Buddhist monasteries throughout North America by the mid-70s. During this same period, Timothy Leary, Ralph Metzner, and Richard Alpert (Baba Ram Das), high priests of America's psychedelic revolution, released *The Psychedelic Experience*,[2] an LSD travel guide based on the 1927 *Tibetan Book of the Dead*.[3] And in 1974 there was E. J. Gold's *American Book of the Dead*, explicitly published not only for the dead, but "for all labyrinth voyagers, all those who wake up dead, deep in one kind of sleep or other."[4] All the above served to initiate thousands of young American seekers after truth into the mysteries of the transit experience, helped along now not only by the wave of spiritual migrations from the East but by a tidal wave of mind-altering drugs. Too, related research into the death and near-death experience as contained in books such as Raymond Moody's *Life After Life*, Robert Monroe's *Journeys Out of the Body*, and the various works of Elisabeth Kübler-Ross created an enormous interest in the exploration of what lies beyond death.[5]

In 1975 a second, culturally more accessible, translation of the Tibetan classic was published. *The Tibetan Book of the Dead: The Great Liberation Through Hearing in the Bardo*, translated by Francesca Freemantle, offered a more accurate title of that sacred text, given that traditional practice involved reading its words into the ear of the newly deceased with the hope of guiding the spirit into liberation from rebirth.[6] Freemantle's teacher, Chögyam Trungpa Rinpoche, points out in his foreword to the book that the word *Liberation* in the title means that anyone coming into contact with this teaching, even in the form of doubt, will receive a sudden glimpse of enlightenment through the power of the transmission contained in its words.[7]

The Tibetan Book of the Dead was, and is, considered by many to be the ultimate do-it-yourself manual on achieving liberation or at least a favorable rebirth after one's death. According to Tibetan spiritual master Sogyal Rinpoche, "In this wonderful teaching, we find the whole of life and death presented together as a series of constantly transitioning realities known as *bardos*. The word *bardo* is commonly used to denote the intermediate state between death and rebirth, but in reality bardos *are occurring continuously throughout both life and death,* and are junctures when the possibility of liberation, or enlightenment, is heightened."[8]

The individual consciousness experiences transit, or the bardo, as a condition of uncertainty, a state of existing between death and rebirth within which consciousness travels, experiencing the unwinding of the mind and its projections of all that has seduced and scared the psyche during its lifetime. Just as in film blanc, transit, according to the Buddhists, can look very much like ordinary life. In a sense, the being's first task is to recognize that he/she has died and is now in the transit world. Transit experiences can seem very bizarre, but the bizarreness reflects our own mental images, just as do our dreams and fantasies. Dreams, reveries, even our moment-to-moment existence are, according to the Buddha, all transit states, that is, states of uncertainty between the death of one idea or self-identification and the birth of another. Seen in this sense, a transit state occurs between each successive thought. At the heart of the transit state, there is a sense of not knowing quite where, or even who, we are, of having lost our familiar moorings, an experience of groundlessness. Like the passengers in *Between Two Worlds*, we try to control our transit by invoking our familiar ways of manipulating experience. When these well-worn strategies fail, moments come of pure confrontation with our naked selves, stripped of the coverings of familiar beliefs and habits. In these moments of nakedness, an unfamiliar clarity is possible, an instant in which we can see our fears and desires as simply the creation of our own minds. By embracing these creations, whether they appear seductive or horrifying, by claiming them as our own instead of denying them or projecting them as existing outside of our minds as threatening demons, we can attain a glimpse of the quality of *suchness* itself, what the Buddhists call *dharmata*—that which is simply the inherent expression of the ultimate reality.[9] With the recognition of our experience as manifestations of mind comes the possibility of rebirth into the peace of enlightenment. If we flee, like the architect in *Dead of Night*, these monsters of our mind return again and again in even more terrifying forms. The Buddhists are themselves very insistent that the transit experience is part of our basic psychological makeup, that *The Tibetan Book of the Dead*, while ostensibly written for the dead, is in fact about life and living, that "birth and death apply to everybody constantly, at this very moment."[10] It is said that the Buddha himself would not discuss what happens after death because such questions are not useful for the living in the search for reality here and now.

Resurrection (1980) is a film that can be viewed as highly informed by the various theories, revelations, and rediscoveries regarding death that were revived or generated during the 1960s and 1970s. The film, like most film blanc, is highly sentimentalized and touching, but marks its modernity in any number of ways. Screenwriter Lewis John Carlino obviously drew much of the film's content from recently published reports of people who claimed to have returned to life from clinical death and from reported experiences of ego death and rebirth during psychedelic trips. The film's imagery draws as well from traditional religious sources, a crucial element of that imagery being the brilliant luminosity that dominates the initial states of the heroine's transit vision. In *The Tibetan Book of the Dead*, this light is referred to as the Clear Light of the Void and is deemed to be the blinding brilliance of pure, unadulterated consciousness, the essence of *total* reality. Resurrection, the act of rising again from the dead, is associated strongly in the film with its implied cultural meaning of the death and transfiguration of Christ, but given timely significance by the depiction of Christ as a woman, Ellen Burstyn in the role of Edna May McCauley. The film utilizes such traditional imagery not to depict the fanciful passage of a soul from here to some heavenly reward, as in past film blanc, but to portray the actual transition of a human consciousness from its ordinary and mostly confused waking state into a state of total clarity, bliss, and absolute unity.

Resurrection is the story of Edna May's experience of transit, her ego death, and her ultimate rebirth into life everlasting. "Life everlasting" should be understood here not as a body, mind, or separate self that lasts forever, but rather as the maintenance of one unified state of awareness across all possible states of existence. In his foreword to *The American Book of the Dead*, Dr. John Lilly writes that

> the human lifespan is designed to carry over and through many different times and conditions. But if the consciousness principle breaks up into forgetfulness, then the chief aim of the purpose of existence—to perfect oneself and become completed man—is lost in the confusion. The answer is simple, and has been known by many esoteric brotherhoods in the entire space of human history and before. The practice of maintaining a connective thread of consciousness between lives, and experiencing a single life with a single principle of consciousness, or permanent I, has been a fact for many thousands of years of material time. Please understand that an expanded lifespan is not for the purpose of amusing oneself with 'immortality'—it is for the purpose of perfection of the self, and it is designed to give one a lifespan of the biblical proportions necessary to accomplish this great aim, of liberation and awakening."[11]

For Edna May, as for most of us, consciousness consists of varying levels of awareness of three states of existence—life, dreams, and death. An auto accident in which she survives but her husband dies introduces into her consciousness an awareness of the fourth state of existence, transit. In the intensive-care unit, her heart stops. She experiences the vision of a long, dark tunnel with a brilliant luminescence at its end beckoning her with its peaceful radiance. Other people are there, familiar loved ones, guiding and encouraging her toward the light. Her feelings of deep peace and total understanding are abruptly terminated as the camera zooms back from the circle of light and she wakens to be told of her husband's death and her narrow escape.[12]

Edna's awakening is a rebirth. Like an infant, she is helpless, paralyzed from the waist down, with the prognosis that she will never walk again. Taken from the hospital by her father, she is to begin her life again with a return to her childhood home, a farm in Kansas. Driving through the desert east of California, they stop at the Last Chance Gas, a ramshackle collection of sheds and shacks operated by a seemingly pixilated old man named Esco Brown (Richard Farnsworth). Esco is the embodiment of crazy wisdom, full of pure life energy, innocent yet experienced, and wise beyond attempting to explain the mysteries of life. A faded sign declares the motto that suffuses his life: GOD IS LOVE AND VERSA VISA.

While filling their tank, Esco shows Edna a two-headed snake. It is at once seductive and repellant, beautiful and horrible, a powerful symbol that asserts the actuality of the miraculous. Edna leaves the Last Chance Gas with the seed of that actuality planted in her recently tilled psyche.

The bleakness of the Kansas autumn is warmed by the presence of Grandma Pearl, Edna's living connection to a time when the miraculous was not so far from everyday life. Grandma Pearl (Eva Le Gallienne) is quick to discover an unusual warmth in Edna's hands after Edna stops her niece's bleeding nose simply by holding her in her arms. The incident revives in Pearl the remembrance of a woman in Macon who died of pneumonia but returned to life after ten minutes. From then on, the woman could heal folks; maybe the same thing was happening to Edna. Grandma Pearl has also heard about the strange tunnel with the beautiful light, and she recognizes the people in Edna's vision as dead friends and relatives.

The sum of Edna's recent experiences leads her to hope that she can somehow heal herself. She spends the winter in a cottage behind her father's house, devoting her entire energy to that end. By early spring, she is taking her first steps, followed shortly by a complete recovery. Unable to identify the source of this healing energy, Edna recalls Esco Brown's sign, GOD IS LOVE AND VERSA VISA, and fixes on the possibility that she can heal others with this power of love. An opportunity appears in the person of Cal (Sam Shephard), the son of a self-styled hellfire-and-brimstone preacher, who is bleeding to death when he is brought to her. Edna does indeed heal him, and they later become lovers.

By summer, Edna is traveling the local countryside, gaining a reputation as a healer for her work with the chronically sick and lame. Two observing scientists invite her to California, where her methods can be studied, but she declines, not wanting to be used as a guinea pig. While many consider her a miracle worker, some, especially Cal's father, view her as a handmaiden of the devil. Cal struggles against these projections of evil, but as his puritanical structures begin to break through his cynical facade he increasingly projects his father-induced fantasies of the Second Coming onto Edna.

With autumn, the fragile domestic arrangement at the farm falls apart. Edna's father, his own conflicted feelings triggered by his daughter's sexual relationship with Cal, angrily confronts Edna and orders her to leave the farm. She returns to California, taking Cal with her. There, after a particularly difficult session healing a woman, Edna reexperiences a transit state, this time seeing her father wandering toward the brilliant white light. Awakening from her vision, she tells Cal she must return to Kansas because her father is dying. Unable to grasp how she can know about her father and increasingly filled with convoluted imaginings of the Second Coming, Cal is pushed closer to his mind's edge.

Back in the Kansas winter, Edna confronts her dying father with all the resentment and fear, sorrow and anger, love and acceptance that she has never expressed. In an effort to break through his stony isolation, she tells him about her vision, about the bright light, the familiar faces, the feeling of well-being and peace. Her attempt to give him hope, to resurrect the faint possibility of rebirth from his cold, loveless world, is rewarded with his final words, "Oh . . . Oh . . . my. The light, Edna . . . the light!"

It is early spring again, and we see Edna framed against a broad, empty field. She is preaching, but we do not see her congregation; they are hidden, situated behind the observing camera. Edna is alone, psychically on another plane. Only the breaking of one final link is needed to set her free completely. The angel of deliverance, riding a motorcycle and armed with a rifle, comes roaring into view in the person of Cal. Possessed by his apocalyptic fantasies, he has arrived to declare the Second Coming of Christ with a blast from his rifle. He fires into the crowd, wounding Edna in the shoulder before being subdued. In the following scene, her shoulder still bandaged, Edna leaves the farm, heading for a new life. In a series of slow dissolves, we watch the farm crumble into dust, a symbol of the final dissolution of Edna's ego existence.

The final scene brings us back, full circle, to the Last Chance Gas as a large motor home is pulling in for fuel. Its occupants are a young couple taking their fatally ill son on a final trip through the southwest desert. From one of the dilapidated sheds ambles Edna, a little older and grayer, a little stranger looking, rather like the former proprietor, Esco Brown. She sends the young couple off to see her cactus garden while she fills the tank and takes that opportunity to show their boy Esco's two-headed snake, dead now, but preserved in alcohol. Again, the possibility of the miraculous is introduced. As the family is about to leave, Edna bends down and embraces the child. We sense the transference of love's healing energy between Edna and the youngster, and we know intuitively that he will live.

Resurrection is about a human who dies and rises again in a transfigured form. Her transfiguration is not sudden, but is a process inaugurated by her ongoing awakenings to the true nature of consciousness. Edna's obligations to the past, the consequences of her life to its present point, must be paid in full before she can realize the benefits of her newly acquired wisdom. Her return to Kansas, to the source of her psychic situation, is also her chance to experience consciously and clarify the ties and attachments that bind her to her past identity. Her connections with relatives, friends, and lover, as well as places and memories, are played out until no longer binding on her. She sees through the desire for possessions and the fear of loss and death that dominate human relationships and instill basic clinging attitudes toward life. Through her experience of the state of transit, she knows that nothing can be lost, not even life. This knowledge allows her to relinquish her ties and attachments, not with ascetic detachment, but with a deep faith in the interrelatedness of all things. Having experienced that which is eternal, she can give without end because there is no end. The healing energy of that knowledge is what she passes to the dying boy. *Resurrection* is a moving rendition of transit as a lived experience touching life at every moment.

Chapter Five

THE POPCORN BARDO—
TIBET MEETS SUBURBIA

Poltergeist

To live in the modern world is to live in what is clearly a bardo realm. You don't have to die to experience one.

—Sogyal Rinpoche

Awareness of transit, as we have seen, is usually associated with altered states of consciousness—a knock on the head, a brush with death, illness, dreams, or death itself. Given the threat of immanent death and destruction that hung over life so palpably in the decades following Hiroshima and Nagasaki, it comes as no surprise that our own worst dream, the "nuclear nightmare" in the form of Three-Mile Island and the toxic disaster of Love Canal, should have elicited from Hollywood its most successful-at-the-box-office treatment of the transit world up to its time.

Poltergeist (1982) is the story of a typical American family confronted with death and the beyond in their everyday lives. Steve and Diane Freeling have provided their family—Dana, fifteen; Robbie, seven; and Carol Anne, five—with a life of unremarkable happiness in a typical suburban split-level home in Southern California. Steve views with pride the look-alike dwellings surrounding his own; a number one salesman of the entire development, he has sold most of the houses in Cuesta Verde Estates. The Freelings were the first to move in; little Carol Anne was born in their home. The healthy routine of their family belies the fact that all is not quite right in Cuesta Verde. Things, in fact, are getting increasingly bizarre: an earthquake singles out just their house to shake, inanimate objects move about at will, the gnarled oak outside Robbie's window tries to eat him, and Carol Anne is sucked into her closet by a strange light and disappears into some coexisting astral plane within the house itself, as the family TV begins to broadcast her cries for help across the higher UHF channels.

Helpless with fear and near hysteria, the Freelings turn to that general panacea of the times, psychiatry, in the person of Dr. Martha Lesh. Although she was trained in conventional psychiatry, her interests have shifted over time from traditional psychology to the study of paranormal phenomena such as ESP, psychokinesis, precognition, and reincarnation. Her initial reaction to the Freelings' plea for help is one of suspicion, for her field is riddled with cranks and sensation seekers. What she finds at their house, however, can only be described by her favorite quote: "The universe is not only stranger than we imagine, it is stranger than we *can* imagine."[1] Objects fly through the air in defiance of gravity, midair flashes discharge objects onto the living-room floor, and the frightened voice of Carol Anne cries for her mother from the television set. But these phenomena pale by comparison with the ghostly procession of diaphanous forms that float down the Freelings' staircase and across the living room, aimlessly wandering spirits, lost to each other and to their surroundings, searching for who knows what. But these restless souls are not the only ones who are lost. Carol Anne is lost, and the whole Freeling family is wandering in a realm for which they have no maps. Their life of ordinary reality and surface normalcy has been shattered, spilling them into a plane of existence where their conventional wisdoms and responses are meaningless. Indeed, the

Freeling home has become the transit world itself. Lest there be any doubt of this, a clear and clever signpost of the territory we are entering is provided in an early scene in which Steve and Diane watch an old movie on TV, *A Guy Named Joe* (1943), a meandering film blanc/transit fantasy about a dead pilot (Spencer Tracy) who returns to Earth as a ghost to supervise his girl's new romance with a young aviator.

Wandering lost in transit, the whole Freeling family is like one being experiencing the realization of its deepest hidden fears and guilt. Robbie is probably the most fearful aspect of the family/being; from the beginning he has feared the oak tree. It is characteristic of the nightmare quality of transit that the tree should animatingly attack him. Dr. Lesh speaks to Robbie's fear and confusion, as well as to his curiosity about death, when she tells him, "Some people believe that when you die, there is a wonderful light, as bright as the sun, but it doesn't hurt to look into it. All the answers to all the questions you want to know are inside that light. And when you walk into it . . . you become part of it forever." Robbie wants to know about the ghostlike people who are wandering through his house and have taken his little sister. Lesh goes on, "Well, maybe some people, when they die, they don't know they are gone. . . . Maybe they didn't want to die. Maybe they'd hardly begun to live yet, or they lived a long, long time anyway, but wanted more life. They resist going into the light, no matter how hard the light wants them." But when Lesh tells Robbie about the spirits who have not recognized their own death, who "hang around, watch television, watch their friends grow old, feeling all unhappy or jealous," she could just as well be describing the feelings of helplessness, alienation, and isolation that haunt so many everyday lives.

The bright light comes into play again when they hear Carol Anne's voice over the television saying, "I'm afraid, Mommy. I'm afraid of the light." Lesh warns Diane, "Tell her to stay away from the light." "But maybe it's a way out!" Diane protests. "It is," Lesh answers. "It is a way out. . . . It's *the* way out. But not for her." Lesh is here acknowledging that the bright light, the same light Edna May experienced in her transit vision, is the Clear Light of the Void set forth in *The Tibetan Book of the Dead*. As a way out of transit it leads to complete and absolute absorption into eternal unity. It must not be a way out for Carol Anne if she is to return to this world.

In a few simple paragraphs under the heading "The Spookiness of the Ego-Mind," the Tibetan lama and teacher Dzigar Kongtrül makes it clear that maintaining an ordinary notion of self, or ego-mind, is the source of our everyday pain and confusion. That this mind controls everything we do but, when examined, cannot actually be found is "somewhat spooky, as if a ghost were managing our home." He finds it a "funny thing" that we never question this ghostliness. "We just assume that someone or something is there. But all this time, our life has been managed by a ghost, and it's time to put a stop to it. . . . If you want to stop being the slave of a ghost, you must demand that ego-mind show its face."[2]

To end the ghosts' management of the Freeling home, Tangina, the dwarf clairvoyant brought to the Freeling home by Dr. Lesh, explains Carol Anne's situation. Carol Anne represents the family's essence, its innocent self with an open mind. She was born in the house and has a special connection with the spirits who are haunting it; she is a living presence in their spiritual but earthbound plane. But, more than anything, the ghosts are attracted to that part of her that is different from themselves—her life force. It is very strong, giving off its own illumination. For the lost spirits it is a light that implies life—the memory of love and home and earthly pleasures—things they desperately desire, but can't have anymore.

It falls upon Diane, the mother, to deliver her baby once again, snatching her back from the transit realm into the human world. Girdled by a cord and guided by Tangina, she must enter that realm through the point of bilocation in the children's closet, retrieve Carol Anne, and return through the opposite point midair in the living room. Steve must anchor the cord and not let go, no matter what. Diane's mission nearly fails when Steve is confronted by his monster, the thing that most frightens him; he drops the cord and almost loses his wife and child. Steve's monster is his willful ignorance; enthralled by his success as a salesman, he does not question his obviously slimy boss about what really went on in the building of Cuesta Verde, about the failure to remove the coffins from the old cemetery before beginning construction. His inability to face the truth about the development and his collusion in its desecration make him unable to help his family until the very last moment, when he accosts his boss and snatches his family from the grip of the doomed house. The horrifying manifestation of Steve's inner fears is, once again, characteristic of transit—that whatever we are unwilling to face during our lives will confront us in transit in its most terrifying form, and that if we are unwilling to accept that form as a projection of our own consciousness and take responsibility for it, no matter how repellant, we will be condemned to suffer it again and again.

Poltergeist draws a timely portrait of the American nuclear family confronting the unknown in their everyday lives. But the unknown is not the unknowable; rather it is what they *refuse* to know. It is Steve's willful ignorance that nearly destroys his family. The spirits that wander through the Freeling family's living room are the souls of the people whose graves have been desecrated in building Cuesta Verde. The Freelings seek guidance in the person of the diminutive Tangina, a student of the paranormal, whose openness to and acknowledgment of other states of being allow her to read the maps of their condition. Science can measure and define phenomena, but its ability to deal with the beyond is greatly circumscribed by its sanctions of what can be considered legitimately scientific. Dr Lesh and Tangina are also limited by the very nature of their role as parascientists, as investigators of paranormal events. In *Eye To*

Eye: The Quest for a New Paradigm, Ken Wilber posits that parasciences are *"not* the same as the transcendental sciences per se, simply because, in virtually all psychic events, the mind and senses are *not vertically transcended*, they are simply *horizontally extended*, by mechanisms as yet unclear."[3] Nevertheless, in her acknowledgment of the Clear Light of the Void, the White Light of Absolute Consciousness, and her implied familiarity with one of the more esoteric spiritual texts, *The Tibetan Book of the Dead*, Dr. Lesh would seem in sympathy with what Carl Jung wrote in his psychological commentary to that sacred treatise: "The *Bardo Thödol* [*Tibetan Book of the Dead*] is in the highest degree psychological in its outlook; but with us, philosophy and theology are still in the medieval, pre-psychological stage where only the assertions are listened to, explained, defended, criticized and disputed, while the authority that makes them has, by general consent, been deposed as outside the scope of discussion."[4]

It is interesting to compare *Dead of Night* with *Poltergeist* and *It's a Wonderful Life* with *Resurrection*. Although the more recent films borrow heavily from contemporary studies and archetypal psychology dealing with death, and while they fully utilize advanced cinematic technology, delivering amazing special effects, their impact on human consciousness is actually less than earlier films. For all its sophisticated imagery and graphic horrors, *Poltergeist* lacks the true eeriness of *Dead of Night*. Its portrayal of transit is so cleverly covered by its technical sophistication that it fails to convey the essential point—that the experience of transit, its bliss and terrors, is the experience of the unraveling of our own minds into their primary components. *Poltergeist* fundamentally suggests that transit is something that happens to people because of things beyond their control. This interpretation is precisely what transit is not. As *Dead of Night* shows so clearly, the apparitions of transit are those that we call forth ourselves, through the processes of desire and aversion, aspects of our own innate ignorance. *Dead of Night* strikes fear in our souls because it speaks directly to the unconscious mind, which is *always* connected to the transit state. In portraying the particular terrors of particular minds rather than the spooks and skeletons of *Poltergeist*, it carries the spiritual power to imbue us with the determination not to be ruled by our fears, lusts, and projections. In that sense, *Dead of Night* functions like some wrathful mirror, forcing us to confront our ego-protecting ignorance.

It's a Wonderful Life also has a spiritual power to inspire, to seek out and engage with the suffering that leads to an end of suffering, to fill the vision of good inside each of us with the energy and clarity of the transit state. Along with George Bailey, we feel that we have had an experience of the spirit, that its luminosity has healed our souls, and that, like George, we are reborn. There is nothing mysterious in the fact that *It's a Wonderful Life* has become America's *Christmas* movie, functioning as our favorite tale of death and regeneration, and appearing endlessly on television throughout the holiday season. Preachy and corny as the film is, it works.

Resurrection, with its high-minded goodwill and compelling special-effects vision of the Clear Light of the Void is compelling; Ellen Burstyn's performance is loving and lovely, and the dialogue is certainly no cornier that Capra's. But somehow *It's a Wonderful Life* touches our spirit in a way that *Resurrection* does not. Perhaps the reason is merely its innocence, in contrast to the calculation that informs *Resurrection*'s goodwill. Capra himself said that his film had more than he put into it, that something happened that gave it a life and a power of its own.[5]

It's a Wonderful Life achieves its own transcendence and encompasses more than the conscious minds of its creators. Like all great movies, it goes directly to the archetypal level of our consciousness and elicits a remembrance—the recognition of a deeply held inner truth. Perhaps its art lies in its very absence of pretentiousness. *Resurrection*, drawn from contemporary life-after-death literature, seems to strive too hard for authenticity. Nevertheless, its portrayal of the transit experience manages to touch our hearts as much as our minds, opening the box-office window to the great transit movies to follow.

Chapter Six

THE BARDO OF DYING

Jacobs's Ladder

Now when the bardo of dying is dawning on me.
I will abandon grasping, attachment, and the all-desiring mind,
Enter undistracted the clear essence of the instructions
And transfer into the space of unborn self-awareness.
As I leave this conditioned body of flesh and blood
I will know it to be a transitory illusion.

—The Tibetan Book of the Dead

In 1990, screenwriter Bruce Joel Rubin gave us *Jacob's Ladder*, a profoundly disquieting but deeply moving film, apparently about a Vietnam veteran having flashbacks. Vietnam (and its real-life sequels, Operation Iraqi Freedom and Afghanistan) was, and remains, an American nightmare. It had indeed the hallucinogenic quality with which it is invested in films. And we were all stoned—on something. For the mainstream it was alcohol, tobacco, and illicit sex. For the counterculture it was marijuana, hashish, mushrooms, LSD, and so forth. And it all appeared each night on television, in living, bleeding color. It was horrifying—a profound shock to the physical senses and to the moral sense. It haunts us to this day, because we Americans can't or won't acknowledge what was done there in our name. It is that willed forgetfulness that has caused our culture to create *Iraqi War I and II:*

Return of the Repressed and its various and seemingly endless sequels—Orwell's infamous War in the East, as depicted in his novel *1984*.

Jacob's Ladder begins with medevac helicopters flying over the Vietnamese jungle. It then cuts to a scene with a platoon of GIs smoking weed. Everyone is stoned. It is hard to know exactly what follows, except that it's horrible and that Jacob (Tim Robbins) is bayoneted through his guts. We are immediately plunged into the bardo of dying, and dying in the worst possible way—in terror, shock, pain, and confusion.[1] It is the kind of death most to be feared—to be plunged, utterly terrified and unprepared, into the process of painful death.

Jacob then awakes in terror from that nightmare of Vietnam. He is now a postman, napping on a subway coming home from work. He looks at least half dead—his skin is pasty, he slouches, and everything about him is flat and numb. Confused, he tries to ask his fellow passengers whether he has missed the Bergin Street station. The passengers, who look uncanny and even subtly horrifying, don't know what he's talking about. There are subway signs, especially one saying "HELL." Jacob is disoriented yet insistent. The train finally stops at Bergin Street and he gets out, only to find the station has been closed and locked up. By now it is clear that Jacob is in transit, that uncertain, porous, space between life and death. There is that uncanny quality, the strange half-light, and the fact that no one seems to recognize him. He has fallen out of time. As he tries to step carefully between the tracks, Jacob is startled by the intensely white light of pure consciousness, but in his fear and disorientation he experiences it as a threatening light from an oncoming train and tries to avoid it.

He wakes again into his postman identification. Here he lives with a woman, not his wife, aptly named Jezebel (Elizabeth Peña). Jezzie is dark, almost always wearing black, amazingly seductive, but possessive. It's clear that their bond is a kind of negative sexuality that keeps Jacob away from his beloved wife and sons, his bond of generative sexuality joined with love. Jezzie embodies the dark feminine, the Black Witch who burns Jacob's treasured family photos in the incinerator so that he can be hers alone.

As a postman, Jacob suffers from chronic back pain. His spine is out of line. Buddhists and Hindus might say that energetically his kundalini is stuck in the lower chakras, from his heart on down, so that his soul can't leave his body by passing up the spine and out through the crown of his head. He can't die. His guardian angel, appropriately enough, is his chiropractor, Louie (Danny Aiello), who has the skill to adjust both Jacob's body and his soul so that he can complete his journey through the transit state of dying and move into the beyond. This is Hollywood, so Louie's angelic identity is made instantly clear through lighting. While Jacob and his environment are both a dead yellow-green-gray, Louie is backlit in brilliant white; a ceiling fixture suggests his halo. He is no ethereal angel, but a powerful and practical guy whose strong hands push and twist Jacob's pain-wracked body into releasing its suffering. One of Louie's adjustments generates another flashback; once again Jacob is in the jungle, under attack. Leaving Louie's office, Jacob is chased by a large dark car.

By now it is clear that Jacob keeps sliding between realities. In some he's in Vietnam, in others living with his wife and family, including Gabriel, his youngest son; in still another he's living in New York with Jezzie, suffering flashbacks. This scenario is a perfect portrait of the transit state—a state of uncertainty wherein our seemingly solid worlds dissolve and interpenetrate. If unprepared, living in innate ignorance, we experience confusion and terror, clinging to what we most tenaciously identify with, even as our lives dissolve. There is both the fear of death as extinction and the feeling of having so much unfinished business; we are just not prepared. In Jacob's case, there are two major pieces of business: the death of Gabriel and the mystery of what happened right before his own death in the jungle. Jacob can't really face his grief over Gabriel's death. He may also feel guilt: we are repeatedly shown the scene of Jacob teaching Gabe to ride his bike and later are shown a twisted bike on the ground. Jacob abandons his family and lives a life of dark sexuality with Jezzie. When he looks at Gabe's picture and finally starts to feel, Jezzie angrily objects to his grief and recaptures his attention. She represents the dark egoic forces of anger, jealousy, and possessiveness that keep us from facing our real situation and choosing the good. These forces are present in ourselves and in the culture. They keep us attached to material reality, constantly striving for more and more, desperate to stave off death. Jezzie keeps Jacob stuck between life and death, unable to commit to either.

In each realm he enters, Jacob is told that he is dead. He can never quite take in the information. Over and over he flees between realms, unable to see the truth of his mortality. After a deep chiropractic adjustment from Louie, he burns up with fever—the hellfire of desire, negative sexuality, and the devitalized self. After collapsing at a party (where a flirtatious palm reader looks at his life line and tells him he's already dead), he is consumed with visions of demons and demonic sex. Jezzie plunges the delirious Jacob into an ice bath; he continues to shift between realms. He finally reemerges in his life with Jezzie in a kind of awestruck, horrified state. He asks her directly, "Am I dead?" She denies it and engages him with her jealousy and possessiveness. It's as though, for a moment, his mind has stopped. He realizes he has no idea where he is or what's going on. Nothing makes sense, and nobody seems really to recognize him.

Jacob is truly unmoored. He begins to make a connection with another vet who is having the same weird experiences and flashbacks, and is also being pursued by people in cars. As his buddy puts it, "I'm going to hell." Almost immediately, as he tries to drive off, the friend is blown up in his car. Jacob is flung to the ground, injuring his spine, and winds up in hospital hell. He is taken deeper and deeper, literally

48

into the bowels of the hospital, which are littered with discarded organs and body parts. There's a feeling of nausea. Again, Jacob is told that he is dead, but again he can't take it in. A doctor inserts a big needle into the space between and slightly above his eyes, what the Hindus or Buddhists would call the third eye, or the eye of the spirit. He slides into yet another reality, one in which his wife, Sarah, and their remaining two sons arrive at the hospital to comfort him. Sarah strokes and kisses him and assures Jake that she still loves him. Sarah represents the positive feminine—she's warm and nurturing, a genuine Earth Mother. Jacob tells her, "I'm not dead. I'm alive." (And indeed, in the love of his family Jacob is alive.) Sarah agrees, telling him, "It's just your spine."

Just when it seems that the hell world of the hospital will destroy Jacob, the angel Louie comes to rescue him. Louie sweeps aside all protests from the hospital demons and gets Jacob out of the hospital and back onto his chiropractic table. While he's readjusting Jacob's spine and hearing about his patient's hellish experiences, Louie plainly tells him exactly what he needs to know. He quotes Meister Eckhart, a fourteenth-century mystic, whom Louie describes as another man who saw hell. What Eckhart realized is that "the only part of you that burns in hell is the part that won't let go." He goes on to say, "If you're afraid of dying and holding on, you see demons tearing your life apart. But if you've made your peace, the devils are really angels freeing you from the earth." After a few more spinal adjustments, Louie is satisfied that Jacob is on his way to healing and sends him off.

Back at his apartment, Jacob opens his Golden Eagle cigar box containing his memorabilia. He is finally ready to face the truth, about the army and about Gabe's death. Soon he encounters a mysterious figure, a self-described "hippie chemist," who may be imaginary, but nevertheless has come to tell Jacob "the truth" about what happened in the jungle. He reveals to Jacob that the military had him invent a powerful drug that brought out intense aggression in soldiers. It was called "the Ladder," because it took men down into their most primal fear and rage.[2] He describes the horrific effects when the Ladder was tried on monkeys and then on Vietnamese prisoners. Eventually, he says, they put a dose into the GIs' rations. The result? "You killed each other." The chemist confesses that he sought Jacob out. "I had to find you. I felt responsible." At last! Someone takes responsibility for his actions, and things start to fall into place as Jacob remembers the events of that day in Vietnam.

Finally, Jacob surrenders. He gets into a cab, gives the driver all his money, and says, "Take me home." He soon arrives at a familiar apartment building and is welcomed by the doorman, who calls him "Dr. Singer." The doorman even offers to help Jacob by "calling upstairs." But Jacob doesn't need supernatural help; he knows how to do this himself. He goes upstairs and looks at Gabe's pictures, finally reconciling himself with his son's loss. Walking into another room, he finds his lost son, Gabe, sitting in a pool of light at the foot of a staircase as his old music box plays Gabe's song, "Sonny Boy." Gabe joyfully recognizes his father. Jacob's confusion and alienation are healed. He is finally recognized; he knows and is known. He reunites with his son in a realm where they have never been separate. Again he hears Louie's words "If you've made your peace, the devils are really angels freeing you from the earth." And indeed, his angel-son becomes his guide as they ascend a staircase (ladder) filled with light, clearly leading to the beyond.

The last scene takes place in a military field hospital. Two medics look at Jacob's dead body and comment, "He looks like he's at peace. He fought really hard, though." The bardo of dying is complete.[3] Jacob has come through panic and confusion to a release from his earthly attachments. We have shared in the dissolution of Jacob's life from the time of his wounding to his light-filled ascension. Over the credits, the tune "Sonny Boy" plays. The implication is not only that ultimately there is no time and no separation, but that loss is apparent, not real. Jacob and Gabe are one. The song even suggests that Jacob has reclaimed his true identity as a son of God, united with the light in a divine reality that lies beyond both life and death. The film's screenwriter, Bruce Joel Rubin, a practicing Buddhist, has said that he based his screenplay on *The Tibetan Book of the Dead*. As we've seen, part of its teaching is that the degree of our awakened essential awareness or of our unawakened innate ignorance—our fear, attachment, and sense of separation—determines a transit experience that can be heavenly or hellish; that through insight and contemplation of our present life, we can prepare ourselves to face the visions of transit with equanimity, recognizing that everything we encounter in life or in death is a manifestation of our own consciousness.

We make our own heaven and our own hell. Louie was right: "If you've made your peace, the devils are really angels freeing you from the earth." When we can recognize our own projections—at any time, in any place—we are liberated.

Chapter Seven

LOVE'S LABOR FOUND

Ghost

Mind creates the abyss. The heart crosses it.

—Sri Nisargadatta Maharaj

Nineteen ninety was a very good year for screenwriter Bruce Joel Rubin. He won a best-screenplay Oscar for a fantasy-romance-thriller, a movie about transit called *Ghost*, starring Patrick Swayze and Demi Moore. Ridiculed by many critics as naïve and corny, it has become an enduring favorite. (In fact, there was a brief moment in hip-hop culture when the expression "I ghost like Swayze" meant "I disappear.") Like so many transit movies, its subject is the two most fundamental concerns of our human existence—love and death.

Most of us agree that love is the highest fulfillment of human life. Whether a spiritual believer or not, we know it intuitively and are drawn to love as a plant is to light. We sense that love is our ultimate purpose— the fullest expression of humanness. Love allows us to transcend the lonely prison of individual existence into a greater, warmer, and sweeter existence of unity with another—"souls yearning to fully meet other souls" could be a spiritual way to put it. Religious traditions tell us that through love we achieve transcendence. Only love has the motivational power to carry us beyond the world of separateness into the realms of unity. Love, the Bible tells us, is stronger than death, Neither goodwill nor good ideas in themselves can achieve much unless energized by the motivating force of love.

The longing for unity actually contains two aspects. Seen from the psychological perspective, the longing is deeply regressive, drawn from the first few months of life when the good mother adores her child and attends intimately to its every need, literally worshiping her infant's body with kisses and caresses. For this mother, her baby is the most precious miracle on Earth. For the baby, the mother is experienced as hardly separate at all—baby and mother form a kind of dual unity. The boundary between them is so thin they are hardly distinguishable from one another. The memory of that effortless attunement to our needs and that adoration and oneness remains buried in the subconscious mind, and as we grow becomes our template for love. We long to be reunited with the good mother, to lay down the burden of our selfhood and the responsibility for our own separate life. We want to feel ourselves as *that* precious and miraculous. Self-responsibility is hard, after all, and often lonely. As the natural boundary between self and other grows with maturity, we acutely feel the loss of the paradise of oneness.

From the mystical perspective, we come into the world not merely naked and helpless, but also "trailing clouds of glory,"[1] that is, with an innate primal memory of unity, of coming from the Source of All, which is the same in everyone and everything. From this perspective, the tragedy of human life is the forgetting of that oneness and the fall into separation, not just from the good mother, but from the Divine Unity itself. As we observe that our human body seems to be separate from our surroundings, we come to believe (and are taught by our society) that our minds are inherently closed and isolated from all others. The Divine comes to seem far away, utterly other, or even like an illusion fit only for cowards and weaklings. Even so, the mystics would say, we retain an inner memory of unity as being the basic truth about life.

But for most, personal love feels like the only way to regain that unity, to transcend our sense of ourselves as limited, flawed, and somehow incomplete. Indeed, the further away Divine Love seems, the more human love seems to hold the only healing for our sense of alienation.

Of course, these two schools of interpretation are forever competing. Each one often tries to invalidate the other. Psychologists like to dismiss the mystics' talk of the lost unity by reducing it to the infantile experience. The mystics understandably resist this reductionism and sometimes prefer to overlook the importance of psychological development. Sometimes they even insist on the literal (not metaphorical) truth of the lost paradise of Eden and make themselves look, to the scientists, like unfortunate primitives. Both these perspectives have important truths, and there is no need to invalidate one in favor of the other. Ken Wilber often refers to the "pre-trans fallacy."[2] This fallacy can go in either of two directions. Freud's error, for example, was to reduce transpersonal spiritual yearnings for unity to prepersonal infantile memories of the child-mother bond. Jung's, on the other hand, was to elevate those natural, prepersonal longings for the good mother to transpersonal status.

For those of us who are not philosophers or scientists, the problems with love seem different. Often love seems elusive or difficult: either we can't find someone to love who loves us in return or the bliss of love soon deteriorates into conflict, boredom, or lack of desire. We find ourselves wondering if love has to be so disappointing or if it is just that we have chosen the wrong person. Even when love feels just right, it brings up the fear of its loss. No matter how much we dream of eternal love, deep inside we know that even the most perfect love will end in one of two ways: either we will experience our beloved's death or our beloved will experience ours. Worse yet, that loss could come upon us in any moment, and nothing we do can prevent that.

All of which brings us to *Ghost*, the story of how two people cope with finding and losing, and then finding again, perfect love. Released in 1990, the same year as *Jacob's Ladder*, the film was initially dismissed as shallow, but it triggered something very deep in the popular audience, winning an Oscar for screenwriter Bruce Joel Rubin. Beneath its inevitable Hollywood emphasis on romance and violence, *Ghost* is about the separation of love itself from the object of love. It is also about the transit journey of a truly good man who needs to fulfill his mission, to complete his karmic task in order to transcend it. Once again we encounter that familiar theme of transit films—that each life has a destiny even death cannot deny. In *Jacob's Ladder* Jake needed to discover and integrate the truth of his own life. For Sam Wheat (Patrick Swayze), the young hero of *Ghost*, the need is to protect his beloved and to express his love fully.

Sam has a great job, a stylish loft, a best friend, Carl (Tony Goldwyn), and a wonderful girlfriend, Molly Jensen (Demi Moore). He and Molly have just moved in together, putting a lot of work into renovating their loft. They epitomize the ideal of romantic love. They are effortlessly comfortable and supportive together and not only love but also appreciate each other's essential qualities. They even have an enormous wooden angel that came in through their window. Molly and Sam are also exquisitely attuned sexually; their lovemaking is so sensuous and romantic that their erotic scene together, performed to the Righteous Brother's "Unchained Melody," has become a classic. This scenario is everyone's dream of romantic love, devoid of conflict and effort.

There is just one tiny problem: Sam can't bring himself to say "I love you" directly to Molly. His response when she says "I love you" is "Ditto." When she confronts him about his evasiveness, Sam gets defensive. He explains, "People say 'I love you' all the time, and it doesn't mean anything." This statement is unlike Sam's usual open-heartedness, and we can see that he has been wounded by love and how he defends himself against that wounding.

Sam is a man haunted by impermanence. He is troubled, and Molly, in her perfect attunement, senses it. Sam confesses that the very goodness of their life scares him, because experience has taught him that just when things seem perfect, somehow they don't last. The skull grins in at the banquet. His fears are confirmed when he sees footage of a plane crash on television, and he morosely speculates, "Things come in threes."

Indeed, Sam's fears are soon realized. He and Molly are walking down a dark street after a performance of *Macbeth*, enjoying their closeness, when Molly asks Sam to marry her. After being initially startled, Sam is thrilled. Life is now just about perfect. Marriage will make their love permanent throughout all time. When Sam turns to Molly, the desired "I love you" clearly on his lips, a mugger attacks them. Sam, with his marvelous physicality, fights with the mugger. A shot is heard, and we see Sam running down the street after his disappearing attacker. Then he turns back and is confronted by a horrifying sight, his own dead body lying bloodied in Molly's arms. When Sam reaches out to his own body, his hands pass right through it. Sam is now a ghost.

What is a ghost? Buddhists suggest that a ghost is a being in an energetic/emotional body, bound to the physical plane by resentments, cravings, or attachments. This state is usually created by sudden or violent death; those who experience it are wrenched out of life so quickly that they have no time to complete unfinished business or prepare for death. Upon dying, they find themselves spirits trapped in the same endless existential setting until they awaken, or are awoken by the supplicating prayers and selfless acts of others, to what must be done to break a seemingly perpetual pattern. They are unable to complete the process of dying and move on to rebirth in a different situation, or they are dead and have been reborn into the hungry-ghost realm, one of six possible realms to which a wandering soul can be reborn if not assimilated into the eternal light. Unresolved attachments prevent their energy body from dissolving into that light. Conventional theory holds that ghosts haunt the people and places they were attached to in life and that as energy or ethereal bodies they retain a tenuous connection to material reality. As poltergeists, they can even affect physical reality in small ways, such as by moving objects or being heard by mediums. At least they can in the movies.

Sam's ghost follows Molly to the hospital, where his body is pronounced dead. He is in shock. As Sam sits in disorientation and confusion, he is met by an inevitable figure in transit movies—a kindly, experienced guide (Phil Leeds) who explains what is actually happening to our hero, that he is now dead and in the transit realm. The old man explains that he himself is a ghost and that his ghostly status is maintained by his waiting to be joined in death by his wife, now in the process of dying—and fighting it—in this very hospital. However, as usual in these films, Sam is not really able to digest this information. He is still too caught up with Molly and his previous life.

Later, we see Molly grieving in their loft, talking to Sam as though he were still present—and he is. This phenomenon is said to be a common one with the grief-stricken and their ghosts. It's as if the dead person's energy body stays around for a while, and the people who have been especially attuned to that person sense his or her continuing presence. Death apparently is not as sudden an event as it is assumed to be. Sam is heartbroken by being so near Molly yet unable to reach her. However, he soon discovers another, even more pressing problem. The man who killed him on the street has broken into their loft, looking for Sam's computer code, and he spies on Molly. Sam follows the man, Willie (Rick Aviles), back to his apartment, where he discovers that Willie has been hired by his best friend, Carl, who has been running a money-laundering scam at the brokerage where he works and where Sam had worked. The street robbery had been a setup, an attempt to get Sam's computer code in order to transfer millions. What's more, Willie is clearly a sexual predator who is fixating on Molly. Sam tries to attack Willie and Carl, but he is just a ghost. He discovers that his superb physical skills are now useless to him, and he has no way to defend his beloved. This dilemma produces a moment of clarity for Sam; he now understands that he must learn, and learn quickly, how to function as a ghost, which means learning how to affect material reality without a material body.

Sam knows where to find a teacher. Back on the subway car he had ridden to follow Willie, there was another ghost (Vincent Schiavelli), who had recognized him as a fellow spook and knocked him around. Sam convinces the subway ghost to teach him how to impact physical objects. As a ghost, he learns to use his mind and emotions, to concentrate his passion—his love, his hate, everything—into his gut, and then focus that energy on his intent. After many efforts, Sam finally succeeds in knocking a soda can across the subway platform. He is learning to be a ghost.

Realizing that he has to find a way to let Molly know she is in danger, Sam comes upon a seedy storefront psychic named Oda Mae Brown (brilliantly played by Whoopi Goldberg, who won an Oscar for the role). To their mutual astonishment, Sam finds that Oda Mae, a classic charlatan, can actually hear him. The two worlds have now been connected. Sam persuades the reluctant Oda Mae (by singing "I'm 'Enery the Aighth I yam, I yam" over and over and over) to tell Molly directly of the danger she is in. At first, Molly is disbelieving and, more deeply, feels cruelly invaded in her grief. For her, the all-but-unbearable fact is Sam's absence, and a bogus message from him feels like the final blow. Nevertheless, Oda Mae, coached by Sam, tells Molly intimate details of their life together, culminating in the word "Ditto." Molly's defenses are shattered, as she begins to realize that Sam must still be present and that life and death are not so separate after all. For a moment, her mind stops and worlds collapse.

Once Sam has succeeded in warning Molly through Oda Mae that she is in danger, he sets out to thwart Carl's financial scheme, which he now knows cost him his life. Through computer machinations and offshore banks, Carl had stolen $4 million and hidden it in a fraudulent account. Sam again manipulates Oda Mae into posing as "Rita Miller" (the name on the fake account) to help him get the $4 million as a cashier's check. He then insists she give the check to some nuns who run a shelter, telling her that only if she gets rid of the check will she be safe once Carl realizes what has happened.

Sam now begins exerting his ghostly powers to threaten Carl, typing the word "Murderer" over and over on Carl's computer. In a panic, Carl turns to Molly, trying to find out what happened to the money. Molly reveals far too much. In his panic, Carl begins to sense Sam's threatening presence. He talks directly to that presence, telling Sam that if he doesn't get the money back, he is going to kill Molly. But Sam is fully into his mission now and is growing more powerful. Knowing what he needs to do and doing it—it doesn't get much better than that. Life—and afterlife—is so much better when we have clarity about what needs to be done and an ability and willingness to do it. In life, Sam, was a really good man, but a bit halfhearted; witness his reluctance to say "I love you" to Molly. And let's face it, the pursuit of money (once you've got your New York loft) seldom feels like a truly worthy purpose; being a stockbroker at a desk in a field of desks just isn't that great. Now Sam has a purpose that calls forth the very best in him—courage and devotion. It has become even more than a matter of life and death.

Sam sets off to save Oda Mae from Carl's henchman Willie Lopez, who bursts into her fortune-telling parlor and menaces her. Sam uses his poltergeist powers to terrify Willie, who, in panic, runs into the street and is killed by a car. Sam watches in horrified recognition as Willie's soul, leaving his dead body, is set upon and dragged down through the asphalt to the depths of hell by black-hooded hell beings. Sam has had an extraordinary vision; he has seen another person's afterdeath experience. An aspect of the cosmic process has been revealed, *and* it is just.

But before he can contemplate this revelation, Sam is compelled back into action, again using Oda Mae to help him save Molly. He brings her back to Molly's door, where through her help he convinces the terrified Molly that he is indeed present. Molly's heart is now completely open, as is Sam's. With that opening they feel their deep longing to touch, one last time. Here is the crux of human longing for the lost beloved— for just one more moment, that moment in which all resistances will drop away, fulfillment will at last come in, and we will be filled up enough to let go. Even that ultrarealist Oda Mae is touched by their heartfelt longing; she volunteers to let Sam possess her body so he can touch Molly one last time. Oda Mae's hands reach out to Molly's, and she turns into Sam. Molly and Sam have one last exquisite dance of touch, filling themselves with eternity, forever in a moment.

The moment is shattered by Carl, who bursts in and threatens to kill Molly and Oda Mae if he doesn't get his money back. He grabs Oda Mae and pulls out a gun, trying to get the check from her. Sam manages to grab the gun away, but Carl retaliates by swinging a hanging hook at him. It slides right through Sam's ghostly body and flies into the window, shattering the glass, which collapses, stabbing Carl through the heart. Once again Sam sees death and the afterdeath. Carl's soul rises out of his body, then turns back and sees his corpse. Sam has a moment of intense compassion for Carl; he knows so well what will happen next. And the hell beings quickly come and drag Carl away screaming. This part of Sam's mission is complete, and not just in the way Sam set out to complete it—by saving Molly and avenging himself on Carl. Sam's mission was complete in the moment he saw Carl die and felt compassion for him, knowing what his fate would be. Sam found out that after all, the universe is just and that he can let go of his anger, even about being murdered and even about his life itself.

But Sam has one more task to accomplish. Appearing now in the body of light he is becoming, he tells Molly fully of his love, says good-bye to Oda Mae, shares one last kiss with Molly, and passes over into the light, leaving Molly with her heart broken open and filled with acceptance. The luminosity is filled with welcoming beings, as they and Sam merge into the light.

Ghost shows us that love is not the same as the object of love. We think the source of love is in the other person, but the true source of love is within our own beings. As Sam becomes a being of light he recognizes his self as love itself. Molly can let go of Sam because she too realizes that in love there is no separation or "other." In love there is no space to separate. There is only the eternal here and now. Their last words to each other are "See you!"—and they do, and always will.

Chapter Eight

THE BARDO OF GRIEF

Truly, Madly, Deeply

Whoever finds love
beneath hurt and grief
disappears Into emptiness
with a thousand new disguises.

—Rumi

That a totally charming, but completely arcane subject—a loving couple separated by death, joined to each other in the transit realm to complete the arc of their life together and fulfill their given destinies—should be repeated twice within a year, is, at the very least, uncanny. Great transit movies are few and far between. *Ghost* in America and *Truly, Madly, Deeply* in England both appeared in 1990. The title for the English entry is taken from a word game the couple, Nina (Juliet Stevenson) and Jamie (Alan Rickman), play to challenge each other's description of how much they love each other. Written and directed by Anthony Minghella, his first film, *Truly, Madly, Deeply* succeeds not only in capturing the elusive quality of the bardo experience, but in showering love upon all things, most pointedly the grieving process. You won't find grief listed as an official bardo in any Buddhist texts, but its essential function in aiding the departed soul on its bardo journey is paramount for both the deceased and those left behind. As author Judy

Tatelbaum wisely writes, "Grief is a wound that needs attention in order to heal. To work through and complete grief means to face our feelings openly and honestly, to express or release our feelings fully, and to tolerate and accept our feelings for however long it takes for the wound to heal. . . . Many of us fear that, if allowed in, grief will bowl us over indefinitely. The truth is that grief experienced does dissolve. The only grief that does not end is grief that has not been fully faced."[1] In *Ghost* we saw the truth of this understanding as Molly and Sam, separated by death, work through their deepest fears and sorrow to achieve a perfect realization of the illusionary nature of that separation. But for *Truly, Madly, Deeply*'s Nina, her cello-playing lover and lifetime partner, Jamie, is dead, and she is alone, in the depths of her grief, barely able to deal.

The camera opens on a red, white, and blue disc with the word UNDERGROUND on it. As the camera pans down, we realize we're at a tube stop in London. It is night, and Nina arises from the depths on her way home from work. As she walks the deserted street, the darkness of her mood and the night spread up each side of the street like high black walls, increasing her sense of isolation. She distracts herself from feelings of loneliness and fear by imagining what Jamie might be saying to her. She mouths his words: "Don't be frightened. I've told you . . . walk in the middle of the road." She feels his presence and it helps. She continues her internal conversation, but it shifts to becoming a conversation held that day with her therapist. We see that she is trying to deal with her grief but is mostly losing ground. At home, brushing her teeth before sleep, she reruns the conversation with her therapist. It is confused in her mind, her loss overwhelming all other things in her life. She reaches up and puts out the light, and the film titles come up, imposed over scenes of Jamie playing the cello and the camera tracking through their house.

The next day at work—she's an accomplished language interpreter—illustrates that Nina has been dealing with her grief by slowly closing down and creating a wall around herself. She is attractive to men—they swarm about her constantly—particularly her boss, Sandy (Bill Paterson), who thinks she needs to get out more, preferably with him. She isolates herself at home as well, in the now rat-infested and falling-into-disrepair flat that she bought against Jamie's advice. But even there she finds a variety of gentlemen eager to "fix things" for her. There is Titus, the Polish handyman (Christopher Rozycki), a noisy plumber (Keith Bartlett), and George (David Ryall), a widowed exterminator who talks to his dead wife. In terms of the bardo realm, these circling creatures could be seen as benevolent spirits, guardians of Nina's well-being. True, they all want something, but what they want is to share their love and bask in the warmth of Nina's great heart. Titus even performs a magical Polish folk dance to drive the rat away. Alas, Nina has pulled completely within her shell. This scenario is not an unusual one. For so many, losing a loved one brings feelings of helplessness and remorse, a sense of lost opportunities, rumination upon words and deeds that might have been, a conviction that one has blown it; and now it's too late to do anything but face the overwhelming grief. She reveals the degree of her suffering at her therapy session as she tries, through a litany of tears, to describe her world. "I'm crying, I'm crying. I miss him. I just miss him. 'Cause he's not there. There's no point in going to bed because he's not there. Or, I'm in bed and there's no point in getting up. It's anger isn't it? It's rage! It's rage! I'm so angry with him. I can't forgive him for not being here. I can't. Oh, God."

Sometimes it may seem that the depths of one's sorrow or grief is beyond our reach, a belief that only serves to increase feelings of helplessness and loneliness. But there are many who hold that we can comfort the bereaved while at the same time helping the deceased. Among them are the Tibetan Buddhist, whose "vision of life and death is an all-encompassing one, and it shows us clearly that there are ways of helping people in every conceivable situation, since there are no barriers whatever between what we call 'life' and what we call 'death.' The radiant power and warmth of the compassionate heart can reach out to help in all states and all realms."[2] In the transit realm, this absence of barriers between life and death, as we saw in *Ghost*, offers the possibility of healing not only from the positive actions and prayers of the living but from an even-closer source, the deceased. That evening, having reached some all-consuming level of sorrow, Nina sits on the floor cradling Jamie's cello, as if embracing Jamie himself. She rises, sits at her piano, and slowly enters the ethereal space of a Bach sonata, one that she and Jamie had played together. Hesitant at first, she gradually becomes one with the music, hardly aware that a cello accompaniment has joined in. The camera slowly pans left, and we, and Nina, see Jamie playing the cello. Tears flow from her eyes as Jamie stops playing and Nina softly mouths the words, "Oh, God."

Nina experiences Jamie's return as a miracle. In the magical world of transit movies, return of the departed, especially to benevolently correct or alter some situation affecting a loved one or ones left behind, is a common occurrence. In the classic years of the film blanc (1941–47) it was a fashion. Today, transit movies, shaped by more culturally sensitive and broadly based sources of information, attempt to respect what might be considered appropriate sociocultural realities, such as the bardo or the phenomenon of the near-death experience. Regarding Jamie's appearance, the Tibetan tradition holds not only that can the living influence, through prayer and ritual, the fate of the departed, but that the departed themselves possess, at least for some period of time after their death, great power—enough to bring them "great suffering or great benefit."[3] So, very quickly, after their powerfully emotional reunion, we begin to see not only a hint of the power Jamie brings with him, but also that he is a truly, madly, deeply very clever and sensitive man who knows exactly what Nina needs. That both his speech and his manner are ironic, sometimes sharply so, assumes the quality of a calculated strategy.

Jamie: I kept thinking—just my luck—die of a sore throat.

Nina: Dying! What's it like?

Jamie: I don't know, maybe I didn't die properly. Maybe that's why I can come back. I don't know. It was like standing behind a glass wall while everyone else got on with missing me. It didn't hurt.

Nina: But where did you go? Did you go to heaven or what? Where do I start? (She presses his body to convince herself that he is real.) Are you here? You *are* here! It's fantastic. Can I kiss you?

Jamie: Yeah!
(*They kiss.*)

Nina: Your lips are a bit cold.

Jamie: They're fantastically freezing. That's one thing I really noticed. This flat is *really* freezing.

For a day or two Nina and Jamie are caught up in the wonder of their reunion. The days stretch to a week. The rat has disappeared (abandoning a sinking ship, afraid of ghosts?). Much to Nina's consternation, Jamie has rearranged all the furniture in the flat and, to her discomfort, insists on keeping the heat as high as possible. With a heavy dose of cabin fever she returns to work, meets up with a pregnant friend, Maura (Stella Maris), and they go to lunch. At the restaurant, they get into a squabble with the manager that appears to be accelerating, when a charming man at another table stands, loudly calls them to attention, and throws an object toward them—a live bird, which flies out the window. This magical intervention breaks the mood of the argument and Nina, Stella, and the young conjurer, Mark (Michael Maloney), leave together. For Nina, magic has again entered her life, a magic every bit as powerful as the return of Jamie, and it will work its spell on her.

Returning home that evening, she finds that Jamie has invited four dead companions, Isaac, Freddie, Pierre, and Bruno, over to watch videos. In a marvelously accurate, inside-the-business routine, they are all, to a man, completely obsessed classic-movie buffs and are massively upset that someone has recorded *Hannah and Her Sisters* over *Manhattan*. Nina confesses it was she, for which Jamie whines disappointedly, "Oh, Nina." We see them, minus Nina, watching David Lean's *Brief Encounter* and trying to decide whether to watch *Five Easy Pieces* or *Fitzcarraldo* next. Ghosts don't need to sleep, and this activity will go on all night. Meanwhile, Nina is suffocating and sweating in an overheated bedroom.

Filling Nina's flat with dead people is just a small part of Jamie's strange behavior. We begin to see a certain pattern in his interactions with Nina, behavior that might be called paternal, demeaning, or judgmental. He assumes what normally might be joint decisions, unilaterally deciding where to place furniture, throwing out the carpets, and refinishing the old wooden floors, in *Nina's* flat. We have been watching Jamie and have sensed the love he carries for Nina, so we cut the man some slack, but we begin to see that he is, out of his emptiness, exercising a thousand new disguises.

The next day, Nina, catching a bus to her therapy appointment, runs into Mark with a busload of young people. It turns out that he has a day job; he is a psychologist, and the bus is filled with a group of his developmentally disabled students. They are all giggling and curious about Mark's pretty lady. He stumblingly manages to ask Nina for a date. At the therapy appointment, Nina brings up a hypothetical situation in which a departed loved one comes back, suggesting that she has read about such a case. She asks if that is ridiculous. The therapist asks, "Is what ridiculous?" We have a couple of rounds of that and close the scene knowing Nina is in good hands. Upon returning home she finds her flat filled with dead people, a full string orchestra, Jamie playing the cello, and even guests—all dead.

Mark and Nina have their date, meeting at the Thames Walk, strolling along the river, attempting to get to know each other. There are a couple of false starts when, to avoid having the shortest date of his life, the magician Mark suggests a way to *actually* get to know each other. Each of them will relate the complete story of his or her life while hopping on one leg to a designated point. Mark goes first. It is pure play, charming, joyful, and effective. Nina is amazed how well she knows Mark when he reaches his designated point. It's Nina's turn. She is astonished at what she reveals, proclaiming, "It's like therapy." The magic is transformative. A short time after her day with Mark, Nina gets a call from Maura, about to have her baby. She wants Nina to be with her at the birth. Oh, and by the way, the father happens to be Titus, the Polish landlord. Nina is there, with Titus, to witness another miracle, birth—to hold a new life and let in an essential message to her beleaguered psyche: "Life is for the living."

When she returns home, the flat is in a shambles. Dead people are rolling up the carpets so that Jamie can refinish the hardwood floors. She is particularly upset with Jamie, shouting, "It's *my* flat, Jamie!" She also tells everyone to leave. *Now!* The dead people file out, and Jamie says, "Satisfied? That was really humiliating." Nina is tearful and at a complete loss. She asks Jamie, "Was it like this before?" She can't remember. She painfully asks Jamie to tell her what their first night together was like: "What did we do?"—a question that could sink the best of us. He answers very slowly, in exact detail down to "and when we kissed it was about eleven in the morning—we were trembling so much we couldn't take off our clothes." Nina's face fully reflects the depth of the love they had, and have now. But? She slowly responds, "I held that baby. It's a life I want. I longed for you." Jamie's answer is to recite, line by line in Spanish, as she interprets, Pablo Neruda's poem "The Dead Woman":

> No, forgive me.
> If you are not living,
> If you, beloved, my love,
> If you
> have died,
> all the leaves will fall on my breast
> it will rain upon my soul night and day . . .
> my feet will want to march toward where you sleep,
> but
> I shall go on living . . .

Jamie asks her whether she wants him to go. She replies, "Never." She leaves the house and goes to her car. Jamie is alone in the flat as all his dead friends reappear. They ask, "Well?" and Jamie answers, "I think so." Jamie has completed his mission.

Nina has driven to Mark's work site. His disabled students are happy to see her; they possess a deeply intuitive sense of the love their friend Mark has for Nina. When Nina and Mark go to his car, she begins to cry, understanding that Jamie has released her. She has kept Mark in the dark about what has been going on in her life. She knows she loves him but has been reluctant to let him totally into her life, especially given her living arrangement with a dead husband and all his friends. As they get into *his* car to go to *her* flat, she tells him that she thinks she is free. "I did love somebody but he died. And I found it very hard to get over it." When they arrive at Nina's flat, Jamie is gone, but there is a fresh red rose in a vase. Life goes on. Mark and Nina settle in. Nina even makes a start at refinishing the floors. And, in an act of accepting the low with the high, even the rat (Squeak) returns.

Truly, Madly, Deeply captures the essence of what Sogyal Rinpoche refers to as the still-revolutionary insight of Buddhism that "life and death are in the mind and nowhere else. Mind is revealed as the universal basis of experience—the creator of happiness and the creator of suffering, the creator of what we call life and what we call death."[4] Only innate ignorance, our desire to see things other than they are, can build the barriers between life and death. Jamie's cold, sometimes callous behavior toward Nina can be seen clearly as acts of compassion exercised as "emptiness with a thousand new disguises." Grief is itself a bardo. It is a state in between the life you had with the deceased person and whatever your next life is going to be. To speak, or even think, ill of the dead is considered bad form. This convention produces an idealization of the deceased that, in a way, distorts grief. Nina holds onto that idealization until Jamie's mission of compassion moves her from it. Ultimately, to live truly, madly, and deeply, we all must surrender our grief. As Dale Borglum of the Living/Dying Project concisely puts it, "As long as we live with unresolved grief in our hearts, grief that has not been transformed into compassion, our lives are lived only partially and death comes too soon. We are all grieving until we no longer feel separate—separate from those we care about, separate from our own true selves, separate from God."[5]

Chapter Nine

THE CORPORATE BARDO

Defending Your Life

Man's prior nature is Spirit, the ultimate Whole, but until he discovers that Wholeness, he remains an alienated fragment, a separate self, and that separate self necessarily is faced with an awareness of death and the terror of death.

—Ken Wilber

Daniel Miller (Albert Brooks) is a stand-up guy.[1] We know that from the first frame of *Defending Your Life* (1991), as we watch him address his work group on the occasion of his tenth anniversary with Foote, Cone, and Belding Advertising. We see a man totally in charge, completely in his element, possessing a witty and engaging way of responding to his audience—upbeat, likeable, and effective. That his sense of humor is self-deprecating ("I'll put myself down before you do") doesn't seem like a big deal. His parting line to them as he heads out to pick up his brand-new BMW convertible is, "You guys are great but I wish I could squeeze all of you into one pretty woman." Just a stand-up guy driving his spanking-new BMW down a busy Los Angeles street, singing along with a CD the popular *West Side Story* song "Something's Coming"—in the next instant he drives head-on into an oncoming bus. Fade out.

The busy corridor of a hospital—attendants push a wheelchair holding a semiconscious Daniel along a ramp; there are literally hundreds of other people being moved in wheelchairs. No, wait, it isn't a hospital, it's a bus terminal, and all these people in wheelchairs are being loaded onto buses headed for Judgment City, a typically American corporate-inspired version of the transit realm, perfectly ordered, pastel-colored settings where everything runs with absolute efficiency, from the top right on down to the vapid deluxe chain hotels where departed souls check in for the duration of their defense of the lives they have lived so they can be assigned to a just and appropriate destiny. True both to the genre specifications of film blanc and to traditional Buddhist teachings, one's transit experience can look very much like ordinary life. It is not too much of a stretch to accept a transit realm that looks like either one's everyday waking reality or one's projections of how the afterlife will appear when you combine the pervasiveness of literal-mindedness and conventional religiosity present in large parts of the general population. In *Life After Death*, Alan F. Segal points out, "That we each get what we think we will get . . . is a frequent statement of American multicultural life. This new ideal has much affected the popular imagination; it was for example, the premise of the film 'What Dreams May Come' [1998]. Even hell is nothing but the self-generated setting of the soul's despair. With appropriate 'therapy' in the afterlife even suicides and sinners can be rehabilitated to partake of whatever heaven they best imagine."[2]

The hostess on Daniel's bus maintains a friendly banter—how wonderful Judgment City is, how much they will enjoy the five days they are here, how fantastic the food is, etc. Arriving at the Continental Hotel, they are met by the manager, who suggests they go to their rooms and have a good sleep. "You have nothing to worry about tonight. Everything will be explained in the morning."

The phone wakens Daniel. It is Bob Diamond (Rip Torn), Daniel's assigned defense lawyer, inviting him to his office after breakfast: "Eat all you want, you won't gain weight!" Daniel turns on the television: a game show, *The Biggest Fear*, challenges contestants to face their deepest anxiety; the weather channel promises an eternal "seventy-four degrees and perfectly clear." He goes down to breakfast and is served instantly with the best breakfast he has ever tasted. A quick trip on the Inner City Transport System brings him to his meeting with the exuberant Bob Diamond, who greets him with the question, "Is this what you thought it would be"?

Daniel: What *IS* it? Is it heaven?

Bob: It isn't heaven. It isn't the other place either. Actually, there is no hell, but I hear Los Angeles is getting pretty close.

Bob goes on to explain that, when you are born into the universe, you're born for a very long time, with many different lifetimes.[3] Every second of every lifetime is recorded. So when you get to the end of a lifetime a panel of judges examines whether you're making progress. The point of the whole thing is that you keep getting smarter—keep growing. He points out that Daniel uses only 3 percent of his brain. Bob himself uses 47 percent, but he adds, "Don't worry about it, everybody on Earth uses 3 percent of their brain. When you use more than 5 percent of your brain you don't want to be on Earth—believe me, there are more exciting destinations for smart people." He explains that everyone on Earth deals with fear: "That's what 'little brains' do. Fear is like a giant fog, it sits on your brain and blocks everything—real feeling, true happiness, real joy."

Daniel: So I'm on trial for being afraid? If you're defending me, who's the prosecutor?

Bob: You'll be prosecuted by Lena Foster. We call her the Dragon Lady. They are going to look at nine days from your life. The trial is only four days. The nine days are episodes from your life that we'll be looking at. Worse comes to worse you'll go back to Earth and try again.

The ever-exuberant Bob then reveals that he had three incarnations on Earth. So far, Daniel has had twenty. As if to reassure him, Bob tells him they've had people who went back a hundred times, but then, in a low key, adds, "But eventually they'll throw you away." In parting Bob suggests Daniel visit the Past Lives Pavilion, where he can see some of the people he has been in past lifetimes.

Does Daniel have something to be fearful about? Don't we all? In his dazzling view of human evolution, *Up from Eden*, Ken Wilber points out: "Men and women . . . have two choices in the face of Death and Thanatos: they can deny and repress it, or they can transcend it in the superconscious All. As long as one holds on to the separate self sense, one must repress death and its terror. In order to transcend the death terror, one must transcend the self."[4] Simply put, the ego is always afraid of its own death and constantly tries to avoid it. But despite his fear of death, repressed in him as narcissism, Daniel doesn't watch the road and runs headlong into a bus. His ego's despair, expressed as self-deprecation, is that it knows its own mortality. Fear, and its activation of the sympathetic nervous system's fight/flight/freeze responses, shuts down the cerebral cortex and higher-order thought. Fear makes us all "little brains." So we can sympathize with Daniel, struggling to hold on to the last thing he really needs, his separate sense of self. Attachment to the ego is yet another aspect of innate ignorance—becoming attached to or identified with our belief structures. "Any attempt to do something about your problems is bound to fail, for what is caused by desire can be undone only in freedom from desire. You have enclosed yourself in time and space, squeezed yourself into the span of a lifetime and the volume of a body and thus created the innumerable conflicts of life and death, pleasure and pain, hope and fear. You cannot be rid of problems without abandoning illusions."[5] A smooth transit is looking chancier by the moment, and four more days in Judgment City is what he's got.

That evening Daniel visits the Bomb Shelter, a comedy club where an onstage comic is putting down the older male patrons by asking them confusing, sometimes off-color, questions and then putting them down with "little brain" jokes. Eyeing Daniel, he zeroes in: "You sir, how did you die?" Daniel's quick response, "On stage, like you!" breaks the audience up, including a beautiful woman, Julia (Meryl Streep), sitting alone at another table. She gets up and introduces herself to Daniel saying, "I know you, right?" Her question is genuine; she has a deep interior feeling of knowing him. When she refers to the standup comic as a good example of humor obviously having nothing to do with brain size, she rouses his already simmering interest. When the comic launches into his version of "That's Life," voicing the lyrics, "That was life. That's how you lived it. Now all you little brains are here to defend it," they quickly leave the club.

Slowly walking through town, Daniel and Julia engage in getting to know each other and quickly realize they're a good fit—they like each other. Julia is open, accepting of herself, easy to be with; Daniel is easygoing and funny, but uses humor both as a positive relational skill and as a defense, a way of belittling himself when he is confused or unsure how to react to his emotions. Julia is very upbeat about her defense strategy. When she tells him that her defense lawyer, Sam, has a "big brain," Daniel replies, "I just came from a world with penis envy. Now I'm in a world with brain envy." When she says that Sam told her she will breeze through to the next level, Daniel responds, "I hope you and Sam are very happy. I'll write to you from hell." In spite of Daniel's self-deprecating behavior, Julia feels strongly attracted to him, feels that she knows him. They part in the lobby of her hotel but both know they will see each other again.

The comedy club scene is interesting in that it sets our protagonist in his milieu, the area that best defines his self-identification (read: treasured separate sense of self) and best allows him to use his finely honed skills. He is, functionally, sharp as a tack, putting down the aggressive standup with a perfect one-liner, the one scene in the film where the character played by the director-star is made truly effective and sympathetic. It even gets him the girl. Now, if only he could trust his feelings. He's had his moment of glory but, as Wilber points out, "There is nothing the separate sense of self can *do* to *actually* get rid of death terror, since the separate self *is* that death terror—they come into existence together and they only disappear together. The only thing the separate self can do with death is deny it, repress it, dilute it."[6]

The next morning Daniel arrives at Judgment Center for the process of examining his life, justifying his fears, and determining his cosmic fate. Bob Diamond is already there, along with the prosecuting attorney, Lena Foster (Lee Grant). Lena appears cold and calculating, and Daniel senses an adversarial relationship between her and Bob, an observation that feeds his rising anxiety.

The presiding judges (Lillian Lehman and George D. Wallace) arrive, and the proceedings commence. Foster opines that Daniel, while a quality being, is still held back by fears that have plagued him lifetime after lifetime, and that he must be returned to Earth to work on this problem. As evidence, she submits from his life record file 11–4–19, a video-like clip of an incident when Daniel was 11 years, 4 months, and 19 days old.[7]

The clip shows Daniel being picked on by a schoolyard bully smaller than himself, while his classmates jeer his refusal to fight. Lena asks, "What sort of feelings came up for you while watching the film?" He responds, "Frustration," but Lena isn't buying it and pressures him to admit the answer is fear. Bob objects, stating that "restrained" is a better word. "He was dignified!" As evidence, Bob calls for two other files to be seen, but neither resolves the issue of Daniel's fearfulness. Back at his hotel that evening, Daniel gets a call from Julia. She misses him and invites him to drop by at her defense the next day when his is over, and they'll have dinner.

The next day's defense goes from bad to worse. Lena switches her prosecutorial strategy from Daniel's alleged fear to what she states is his history of poor judgment. Video clip 24-2-16 shows Daniel blowing an opportunity to become a multimillionaire by turning down an experienced friend's strong recommendation to buy Casio stock before it became the largest producer of timepieces in the universe. His rationale: he didn't think the Japanese knew about precision. Another clip, 29-4-5, shows him role-playing with his then-wife, rehearsing his absolute decision to refuse any raise offered him that is under $65,000. On the following day, with his real boss, he caves immediately for $49,000. The prosecutor states that she has compiled 164 misjudgments over a four-year period. She rests her case.

After his proceeding Daniel wanders into Julia's defense. A clip is being shown. It is Julia running from a burning house carrying her two children to safety, an act of true courage. But wait; she rushes back into the flaming building and in less than a moment comes out with the family cat. The lights come up, and everyone is positively aglow with approval; it is clear that even the prosecutor is feeling good about Julia. She and Daniel leave together, and she suggests a visit to the Past Lives Pavilion. When you place your hand on a plate in a booth, a past life is projected on a screen in front of you. Julia sees herself as Prince Valiant, a knight in armor; Daniel sees himself as an African native being pursued by a lion, or as he puts it—"dinner." Daniel asks her how she died. She is hesitant, because embarrassed; she tripped, hit her head, and fell into the pool. They are both defending their lives the next day, so they return to their hotels after making a date for the following evening. Everything Daniel has learned about Julia in the past days has increased his love for her. For Julia, Daniel is someone she feels she has known forever, that he is already a part of her. They part with a kiss, long and intense.

The third day of Daniel's defense doesn't go much better. Bob Diamond's efforts to cast Daniel's behavior in a positive light are mostly offset by Lena Foster's use of the film records to bolster her position that Daniel is essentially fearful and indecisive. That evening he and Julia have dinner together at an Italian restaurant. The food is, of course, outstanding, but they are more interested in each other—that is, until Lena Foster and party arrive and Daniel's anxiety level skyrockets. Julia tries to calm him down, but nothing works and they have to leave the restaurant. When they get to Julia's hotel they sit on a couch and share what they are experiencing with each other. Julia had never expected to have feelings like this; she is completely surprised. Daniel is having the same experience and comments, "And where do we find it—in the pit stop." Julia then invites him to spend the night with her. He tells her that he wants to because he feels the relationship is already better than any sex he has ever had, but he "doesn't want to screw it up." He continues talking from his fear: fear that she is moving ahead of him, fear that they are not going to the same place, but mostly, fear that if he makes love with her and then they are separated he will miss her forever and ever. He goes on, "I've been defending myself for so long . . . I just don't want to be judged anymore." To all Daniel's doubts and fears Julia responds with a simple "I love you."

On the final day of Daniel's defense Bob Diamond makes clever use of the clips to demonstrate Daniel's risk-taking capacity, but his efforts fall short of Lena Foster's bombshell when she plays a scene of his previous evening with Julia, in which he, with what Foster believes is his same lack of courage, declines Julia's invitation to her bed. The ruling is that Daniel will return to Earth. Meanwhile, Julia is judged worthy to move on. Before saying goodbye, Diamond attempts to comfort Daniel with the knowledge that the court is not infallible, and the fact that Foster won doesn't mean she is right. Daniel remains disappointed. He is to return to Earth for another incarnation. His lawyer's last words are, "You won't remember any of this."

We see Daniel, moving like an automaton, boarding a bus. A number of buses are lined up receiving passengers for transporting to their next stop in the cosmic order. When they are full, the buses leave the terminal, pulling out in a straight line. A very disheartened Daniel can barely look up but does, and there, two lanes across from his own, he spies Julia on her bus. He shouts and she looks up and excitedly calls his name. Daniel rises and using all his strength forces the moving bus door open. With alarms sounding, he leaps off the moving bus, crosses the path of another speeding bus, reaches Julia's bus, leaps on, grabbing the corners of the passenger door as Julia, working inside, helps him to force the door open. They embrace to the sound of whistles and sirens. Daniel's judges, watching the telecast of these happenings in their chambers, are amazed. Bob Diamond pipes up to Lena Foster, "Brave enough for you?" The judges render the final verdict, "Let him go."

Daniel has just completed a Hail Mary pass. He and Julia will move together to the next level of their cosmic existence. In a way his accomplishment can be seen as hitching his wagon to a lucky star. It was clear from her first appearance that Julia was moving up. It was equally clear that Daniel's promotion wasn't as certain. It was, in fact, unlikely. But Julia, it seems, intuited all along that he was meant to be part of her destiny, "the mate that fate had her created for." His destiny, however, realized by his last-minute play to avoid losing her, was a force driven again by his fear—fear of being returned to Earth, fear of being alone, fear of losing Julia. In a way, nothing seems to have changed, and their relationship doesn't really instill a sense of success, because it has, so far, failed to generate and evolve any mutual insight, the stuff of true growth. The essence of the transit film is to show characters learning and developing, mastering their limitations in an essential way. What happens in *Defending Your Life* gives us a number of superficial scenes that fail to provide a context for Daniel's courageous move at the end. At best, Daniel and Julia have provided a missing piece for each other, perhaps the piece that leads to a deeper level of self-awareness, perhaps even a deeper sense of perfect unity. Let Wilber have the final word: "Only in the superconscious All, in actual transcendence, is the death terror uprooted, because the separate self is uprooted as well. But until that time, *'consciousness of death is the primary repression, not sexuality.'*"[8]

Chapter Ten

RECURRENCE, SALVATION, AND THE BODHISATTVA WAY

Groundhog Day

The life of one day is enough to rejoice. Even though you live for just one day, if you can be awakened, that one day is vastly superior to one endless life of sleep. . . . If this day in the lifetime of a hundred years is lost, will you ever touch it with your hands again?

—Zen Master Dogen

If a totem animal were to be designated for the phenomenon of transit, surely it would be the groundhog. As popular folk and weather lore goes, if the immortal groundhog, Punxsutawney Phil, emerges from its barrow in Punxsutawney, Pennsylvania, on February 2 and sees its shadow, it will return to its barrow and winter will continue for six more weeks. Such a prediction of endless winter and avoidance of the shadow side of one's own nature is the basic premise of the 1993 romantic comedy–fantasy *Groundhog Day*. Not immediately a box office hit, the film had what the industry refers to as legs, and its title has become a cultural synonym for being caught up in an unsatisfactory, pointless situation that occurs day after day after day. Most of us have had our Groundhog Days—not even an endlessly painful time, but an unendingly

81

boring and banal situation that keeps happening again and again and again. The feeling of being trapped becomes unbearable; awakening to the prospect of another day just like yesterday yields nothing but despair.

Groundhog Day is a movie about a bad-enough man—selfish, vain, and insecure—who becomes wise and good through timeless recurrence. Like *It's a Wonderful Life* and *A Christmas Carol*, it is about a man whose experience of a break in the time-space continuum allows him to harvest the wisdom of a thousand well-lived lifetimes within a single day. True reality is revealed to contain a perfect present; each instant unfolds a fresh Buddha field of opportunity to awaken us to our true nature, which turns out to be inherently loving and turned toward the light.

Phil Conners (Bill Murray) is the weatherman at a Pittsburgh television station. He is both preeningly vain and fundamentally insecure. We first see him gesturing in front of a blank blue screen, seemingly conjuring up weather fronts. He speaks as though he knows the upcoming weather with godlike certainty—as if his gestures can literally call up the weather. Phil is a walking ego. Like any ego he wants two things: first, to be universally appreciated without having to give anything in return, and, second, to control his life so that he gets exactly what he wants and avoids everything he doesn't. He imagines that if he had those two assets he could run his world (and its weather). Snide and witty, he barely veils his contempt for his audience, or for himself for being no more than a weatherman in Pittsburgh, not even a major market, for God's sake! His shame about his career is revealed when he confesses to his fellow anchor, in reply to her humiliating question, that his upcoming assignment will be the fourth time he has anchored the Groundhog Day festivities. Basically, what Phil wants is to be recognized—all the time and by the right people. His self-esteem is so fragile that he needs constant admiration to have any good feelings about himself, and without that he collapses into whining and self-loathing, projected outward as contempt and hatred for others. He needs to have his sense of being special reinforced by everyone, yet he treats everyone with disdain. For him, people are "morons" and "hicks," exemplified by the citizens of Punxsutawney. To have anything to do with such people, much less with the whole ritual of rodent weather forecasting, is utterly humiliating. As he contemplates the prospects of anchoring yet another unbearable Groundhog Day celebration, it becomes clear that he wants nothing so much as to escape from this place where he can find nothing to feed his narcissistic sense of being special.

Phil's companions on his journey to Groundhog Day are Rita (Andie MacDowell), his new producer, and Larry (Chris Elliott), the cameraman. We first see Rita playfully gesturing in front of the blue screen, and we watch her emerge on the monitors as a kind of goddess arising from a whole continent of clouds. Rita and Phil's mutual attraction is evident, but Phil fends her off with sarcasm. Nevertheless, her appearance in his life is like a sun rising, shedding rays of pure goodness into the darkness of his narcissism and insecurity. She is the Good Goddess, whose inspiration brings the hero through to wisdom and fulfillment. She is perfectly incarnated in Andie MacDowell with her cloud of long dark curls and glowing skin—angelic innocence and divine good sense. Rita is repelled by Phil's narcissism and pettiness, but she continues to remain engaged with him. She even forestalls his objections to staying in a Punxsutawney hotel by reserving a room for him at a charming bed-and-breakfast. As we will see, Rita comes to embody the spirit of love that inspires Phil on his transit journey. In each transit film, the hero, like Dante, has a Beatrice—a benign spirit whose love carries him forward. In *Jacob's Ladder*, it is Jake's friend, the angel-like Louie. For Dorothy in *The Wizard of Oz*, it is the good witch, Glinda. And of course, who can forget Clarence, angel second class, in *It's a Wonderful Life?*

In spite of the promise contained in Phil's meeting with Rita, most of his Groundhog Day is vaguely awful. He wakes up to a clock radio playing Sonny and Cher's "I Got You Babe," followed by two inane disc jockeys bantering on about the weather. It is cold and gray outside, and an oompah band is playing "The Pennsylvania Polka." Phil is met on the stairs by a hearty gentleman offering a banal comment about the weather. The breakfast room doesn't have cappuccino or "even a latte." When he goes out into the street, he is accosted by the unbearable Ned Ryerson (Stephen Tobolowsky) trying to sell him insurance. He steps off the curb into a puddle. By the time he gets to Gobbler's Knob for the groundhog ceremony he is seething with resentment. Nothing is going his way. After delivering a sarcastic sound bite on the Groundhog Day ceremony, he refuses Rita's request for another take, "this time without sarcasm," and storms off. Like *It's a Wonderful Life*'s George Bailey, all he wants is to "shake the dust [or in this case, the slush] of this crummy town off my feet." He rushes to the van, determined to get away from this ghastly place. But fate intervenes. Despite his own weather predictions, it turns out that a storm closes the highway. Phil is incredulous; after all, as he says, "I make the weather!" He confronts the highway patrolman at the roadblock, making his TV gestures of calling up weather fronts, but to no avail. He has no choice but to return to Punxsutawney and spend yet another night in the same small-town bed-and-breakfast. After dumping his frustration on Rita and Larry, he sulks off to his room. He wants to take a shower, but is shocked with cold water. Finally this frustrating Groundhog Day comes to an end. And, in a sense, Phil himself has come to a dead end; his wishes for high-quality affirmation and control of events have been frustrated, his narcissistic rage has no satisfying outlet, and now he can't even escape Punxsutawney. His only source of hope is that somehow tomorrow will be better, will offer a new chance at fulfillment.

Imagine Phil's horror when he wakes up the next morning and discovers that Groundhog Day is happening all over again. The clock turns six a.m., the radio starts playing Sonny and Cher's "I Got You, Babe" (surely the nadir of mindless pop hits), the two annoying radio announcers have the same idiotic conversation all over again, *and* he encounters the same man on the stairs that he met yesterday. He reenters the same dining room, where he is met by the same sweet little lady inquiring again whether he slept well. Ned Ryerson pounces on him once more. When he steps off the same curb, he steps into the same puddle. As he approaches Gobbler's Knob, "The Pennsylvania Polka" is blaring all over again. Phil is appalled. On its quest for security and positive self-reflection, the ego constantly seeks novelty, seeks to move out of the unsatisfactory present, with its quality of emptiness and insecurity, into a possible future filled with real and lasting gratification. Hell, for the ego, is the endless quotidian reality, a living death (if death is assumed to be the condition of having no more possibilities, no more attractive future to aspire to, no more glamorous and knowledgeable audience to be applauded by, no set of maneuvers by which to escape a state verging on panic). Phil is consumed by his own need for admiration; other people are at best instruments to get the recognition he craves, potential sources of high-quality validation (nobody in Punxsutawney qualifies) or "morons" who have nothing he wants and so are worthless to him or even obstacles to his grandiosity. Profoundly cynical, lost in bitterness and the innate ignorance of pride, he is alienated both from his own spirit and from humanity itself.

In Phil we see graphically the unpleasant underbelly of ego— its utter selfishness and need for constant support, while it is all the while promoting its unearned grandiosity. And who better to play Phil Conners than Bill Murray, who can embody that combination of bitter anger, self-pity, and wounded esteem better than anybody? Murray's persona is that of a rueful everyman. Indeed, if we're really honest about ourselves, we are much more like Phil than we would like to think. We too are insecure and narcissistic—that's the nature of the ego. Because it is based on nothing but pictures from the past, the ego can never be truly secure in the present. Because our egos are entirely self-preoccupied, other people are nothing but mirrors, whose only purpose is to reflect ourselves in a way that makes us feel either better or worse. It is hard to admit how much like Phil we are. Truth is, most of us are just a bit better at concealing our narcissism, selfishness, and insecurity than he is. We have learned to behave better, if only because we've been trained to think that the pretense of niceness, good manners, and sympathy will actually enhance our self-image and get us more of that admiring reflection from others. It is just another strategy for achieving security and positive esteem in that better future that always lies just ahead. For the egoic self, the daily dailiness is hell—but there's no set of maneuvers that will get us out of here, no hope for a better future. This is it!

So we can all relate to Phil's growing horror and despair as he realizes that *every* morning he wakes up in Punxsutawney to the sound of Sonny and Cher's "I've Got You, Babe" and the same chatter from the radio guys. It gets even worse when he has to deal with the same hearty fellow on the stairs, the same little old hostess inquiring about his sleep, and the same ghastly encounter with the garrulous Ned Ryerson trying to sell him insurance. Every day is just the same. It is Groundhog Day, over and over again. Every day Rita and the cameraman are there to film the emergence of the groundhog Phil and his weather prediction. Every day an oompah band is playing "The Pennsylvania Polka." Charming it's not. Phil understandably muses about a wonderful day he once had on vacation in the Virgin Islands, eating lobster and drinking piña coladas with a girl he just met, and wonders why, if he had to get one day over and over, it couldn't have been that one. Instead, he's stuck in Punxsutawney with a bunch of hicks and a rodent whose weather predictions are more popular than his. This *must* be hell.

Well, not exactly. Actually, he is in the transit state. Remember that transit represents a state of uncertainty, a gap in what passes as the ordinary appearance of events in our usual waking consciousness. In transit, experience presents itself as discontinuous and slippery. The march of time has ceased moving with relentless logic from the past to the future. This gap can be incredibly frustrating for any ego, much less one as fixated as Phil's: to have no future, to be powerless, never to escape the suffering of your present. And yet, gaps have been described as places where "we may receive a glimpse of the light of reality."[1] The experience of this gap is generally preceded by a sense of absolute contraction and conflict in which contradictions reach their maximum intensity. One is in a state of complete exhaustion.

Phil complains to Rita about being stuck and expects her to do something to help him. After all, she's a producer and he's "the talent." She is unimpressed by his dilemma and instead points out his self-involvement, quoting a poem by Sir Walter Scott (hardly the fashionable poet of the intelligentsia!), predicting that he will go down to death "unwept, unhonor'd, and unsung."[2] She's right. Phil has accomplished nothing that will benefit anyone, not even himself. His grandiosity and demanding selfishness alienate him from everyone. No one respects him, not even Phil himself. As Phil realizes he can't escape from Groundhog Day, he casts about for a way to cope with his situation. His sense of himself has been dealt a major blow—he can't get unstuck. He is so outraged that he should have to stay in Punxsutawney; he is so special, so much better than that. One night, drinking at the bowling alley with two local guys, he attempts to convey the immensity of his problem to them, saying, "What if the same thing kept happening over and over, and nothing you did mattered?" One of the guys, staring into his drink, responds, "That sums it up for me."

Phil soon realizes that he is free to engage in all possible self-destructive behaviors, since there are no consequences in time; the next morning he'll wake up to Sonny and Cher, and the events of the last "today" will be as if they never happened. He uses this freedom to indulge himself in cholesterol, sugar, and tobacco. He gets sadistic pleasure out of shocking Rita with his unrestrained gluttony and abandons all traces of self-restraint. At first, this behavior provides Phil with a certain bitter satisfaction, but the novelty of this spurious freedom soon wears off. Still, cynic that he is, he continues to play life as a nasty game of humiliation. He collects information about people as he meets them again and again, and later uses it to manipulate them, realizing they have no memory of ever meeting him before. His basic game is to collect information to sucker people in, to make them believe he is somehow deeply and magically in tune with them because he seems to know them so well. While having sex with a woman he has seduced using these tactics, Phil momentarily recognizes that he actually loves Rita, but quickly turns that realization into another one of his ploys for seduction. He finds out Rita's taste in cocktails, her love of French poetry and the mountains, her toasts to world peace, and uses these facts to present himself as the man of her dreams, pretending a soul attunement he can't really feel. However, his ploys never work with Rita, who is just too sensible and good to fall for his line. Day after day ends with her slapping him in anger and disgust. Even his game of seduction is a failure, and every morning begins again with Sonny and Cher. He will never get Rita into bed, and it is always Groundhog Day.

Phil's despair deepens, and he becomes suicidal. He thinks the only choice left for him is to die and put a stop to this endless day once and for all. He also decides he needs to kill Phil the groundhog as well, sensing their fates are connected. After stealing a truck, he drives himself and the other Phil off a cliff, but to no avail. Day after Groundhog Day he attempts to kill himself—electrocuting himself with a toaster in the bathtub, diving off the town's highest building, standing in front of a truck—and day after day he wakes up to "I've Got You, Babe" and the two inane announcers. He is unable to make anything happen, not even his death. Nothing will ever change.

If we can admit it, most of us have had moments (or even years) like Phil's, feeling trapped in the endless routine of a long marriage, diaper changing and three a.m. feedings, a boring job, another holiday with the tedious relatives, the same commute every day. Our spouse's love has long since lost its marvelous quality, and the appreciations we get from our colleagues no longer count toward making us feel special. We realize how little control we have over the seemingly endless series of boring and frustrating events. Of course, our tendency is to blame our circumstances for how trapped we feel and to long for a different life with more beautiful and satisfying relationships, one in which all these tedious and painful events wouldn't keep happening. "Somewhere over the rainbow," we think, lies another, truer life. But right now, it is always Groundhog Day. Our ego's dream of every-flowing delight has turned into a nightmare. Nothing works.

And when we really face the lack of choice, the way that reality just *is*, utterly uncaring of our egos' preferences, most of us either go Phil's way, delighting in petty meanness as a way of releasing our tensions, desperately trying to escape, defending against despair with cynicism and fantasy—or, just maybe, the gap opens wider, even despair falls away, and we have a glimpse of spaciousness as the thinking, scheming mind stops. In that state there is nothing to do but to accept our life just as it is, not because that's a good thing to do, but because we deeply realize we have, in fact, no choice. It takes a lot of Groundhog Days, but Phil begins to get the point. He knows he wants to be free, and he knows he can't change the fact that it is always Groundhog Day. Here is his core dilemma.

Indeed, it is everyone's core dilemma. All of us are stuck in our own personal Groundhog Days, endlessly repeating the same patterns, always asking ourselves, "Is this all there is?" It seems that it takes a lot of repetitions to begin to wear down our egos, to convince us finally that our dream of endless novelty and permanent gratification is never, ever going to come true. We cling to that dream with such tenacity because, like Phil, we believe that we *are* that ego and that without those dreams life would be unbearable. Lacking any real connection to Being, ego provides the only ground and the only hope we have. We don't give up easily. Round and round we go on the wheel of life and death. In this situation, where is there any freedom, any real selfhood? We are desperate to get out of here. We look to affairs, sports cars, gurus, trips, or medications to escape our predicament. But as they say in Alcoholics Anonymous, "Wherever you go, there you are." Nevertheless, as days and years go on, the alternations of gratifications and frustrations begin to grind the ego down, and just giving up is very tempting. Our dream of freedom seems lost.[3]

Eventually, Phil hits bottom. All his strategies have failed, and he is still here in Punxsutawney. Nothing he does makes a difference. Finally, he just tells Rita what's happening to him—not as a ploy to get anything from her, but simply out of a need to communicate his experience to another human being. Sensible girl that she is, Rita is initially skeptical, but Phil's accumulated knowledge about their situation eventually convinces her. She resolves to spend the day with Phil so she can observe for herself, be a witness for him. She offers to meet him in his world, as an act of compassion.

Phil and Rita spend a magical day together, culminating by sitting on Phil's bed while he teaches her to toss playing cards into a hat. She asks him, "Is this what you do with eternity?" In the growing openness, which is the gift of his helplessness, he acknowledges the truth of what she says and adds, "That's not the worst part. The worst part is in knowing that tomorrow you won't remember me, and you'll treat me like a jerk again. I am a jerk. And it doesn't matter." Eventually Rita falls asleep, while Phil reads her poetry. His desire for her is palpable, and so is his growing love for her as a being.

And the next morning he wakes up to Sonny and Cher. But now Phil is beginning to change. He takes to heart Rita's suggestion that an eternally recurring day isn't necessarily an awful thing. "It's all in how you look at it." Recognizing there is no escape from his situation, Phil begins to use his life as an opportunity to work on himself. Rather than just expecting admiration for his ego's features, he decides to invest real effort into learning to play the piano. Every day seems like the first lesson, but, in fact, day-by-day Phil is progressing into a competent musician. He also takes up ice sculpture, an art form perfectly suited to small-town Pennsylvania in February. Working with the situation at hand, he begins to find that situation workable. He starts to make what might be called "experiments in compassion." He tries to see what underlying needs other people are trying, in their distorted ways, to express, and attempts to fulfill those needs. He manifests an honest curiosity, not based on manipulation, and begins to emerge from his narcissistic self-preoccupation. Recognizing that he can do nothing for himself, he becomes interested in whether he can do something for others. He meets and befriends an old beggar and tries, night after night, to save his life. Time and again he fails. Again his sense of being in charge is exposed as fallacious. The old man's destiny seems unchangeable, no matter what Phil does. So the remnants of his wish for control are thwarted; the only choice left is simply to surrender to what is, to a state beyond hope or despair.

If we are lucky, we can follow Phil's path. We can give ourselves to some inner discipline, whether it is tai chi, sitting meditation, painting, or even ice sculpture. What matters is the acceptance of repetition. One traditional example compares the practice of meditation to a bird that drags a silk scarf across the top of a mountain; the mountain of ego wears away so slowly, and yet the only thing to do is to keep drawing the scarf over it day after day. In meditation (or any discipline), it is the willingness to face the moment and the self just as they are and to confront the boredom, discomfort, and dissatisfaction the mind produces. Little by little, the scarf wears away the mountain, and so with Phil. We can only imagine how many repetitions of Groundhog Day it must take for him to become so proficient on the piano or to achieve such beautiful ice sculptures.[4] It is just that there's nothing else to do, really. He's found what the American Buddhist nun Pema Chödrön calls "the wisdom of no escape."[5]

Phil begins to find satisfaction and even happiness in simply doing his dharma, the naturally unfolding work he is given to do in order to become who he essentially is. Each day he catches the same kid falling from a tree; every day he saves a local politician from choking. He rescues the same women from a flat tire and learns to have a spare tire and jack at hand. He takes a piano lesson. Phil has found a sense of freedom in simply doing what is his to do, over and over, for the first time. Like Sam Wheat in *Ghost*, he knows from within what he has to do and is willing and able to do it. He is giving up on *how he wants it* and is falling in love with *how it is*—always different, always the same. He has reached a state even beyond acceptance, a state of gratitude for his life, just as it is and, most importantly, has broken his helpless identification with his ego. As Tibetan Lama Dzigar Kongtrül explains it,

> Egolessness is the true state of both self and phenomena. Egolessness of self is the realization that there is not a solid, singular, permanent self found within or aside from form, feeling, perception, mental formation, and consciousness; this 'self' is nothing more than a concept that we impute upon these various aggregates that constitute our experience. In this way, ego lacks even a relative existence. Egolessness of phenomena is the realization that all phenomena are interdependently originated, which means that they do not possess an independent, objective existence. They only exist in a relative way.

When we realize their true mode of existence—emptiness—we realize the egolessness or selflessness of phenomena.[6]

And it is another Groundhog Day. This time, when he steps in front of the camera, Phil opens his heart in gratitude for the warmth of the hearts and hearths of the people of Punxsutawney and wishes for nothing more than "a long and lustrous winter." Phil's personal will is now united with the will of reality itself. He begins to realize the wisdom quoted by Jack Kornfield, a Buddhist teacher: "Want what you have and don't want what you don't have. Here you will find true fulfillment."[7]

And fulfillment is what Phil does find. He saves people, plays keyboards in a band, and sculpts ice. And at the end of one of those Groundhog Days, he finally opens his heart fully to his love for Rita, a love based not in trying to get support and admiration for his ego, but in his profound awe at meeting another being, one who embodies goodness itself. Phil is becoming a bodhisattva, a being whose whole purpose is to embody love and realization for the benefit of all. And not a grandiose bodhisattva—he does small things in a small town, yet every act, repeated time after time, becomes a meditation on love and the unity of all. Phil learns to act without attachment, because he knows that tomorrow Groundhog Day will happen all over again and that none of his actions will matter. Yet in the face of that realization, he saves people and plays keyboards in a band. And day after day he loves Rita, without hope and without agenda. He knows he can never succeed in seducing her, but still he is willing to love her, without hope of return. More and more, he senses her nature as goodness, and it is that goodness and purity he's drawn to.

At the end of one Groundhog Day, Rita and Larry come into the annual Groundhog Day party. Rita hears from several townspeople about their heartfelt appreciation for Phil's good deeds. She sees him playing keyboards in the band and is touched by his music. (There is a moment when Phil sees her watching him and lifts his Blues Brothers shades to show his vulnerable self to her.) Phil is no longer that guy who is bound to die "unwept, unhonor'd and unsung." He has become someone necessary to the life of the town. Rita is increasingly moved by his genuine goodness, and when he is being "auctioned off" for charity, she bids $338.84, everything she has, to buy him. Smart woman! A good man *is* hard to find.

Phil is overwhelmed by Rita's gesture, and yet the transit state has taught him not to cling. He simply gives his love to her and demonstrates his deepest feeling by creating an ice sculpture of her. His love enables him to capture the essence of who she is. He knows that the sculpture's beauty will dissolve, but he no longer even cares that tomorrow everything will be gone. His moment of complete freedom comes when he looks into Rita's eyes and declares, "No matter what happens tomorrow, or for the rest of my life, I'm happy now. And I love you." Phil has come into the present and finds it complete. He falls asleep with a sense of fulfillment.

And wakes again to Sonny and Cher, but this time it's different. The announcers go on to a different topic, and when Phil turns his head he sees Rita sleeping beside him. He is incredulous. Something truly different is occurring, and, as Phil says, "Anything different is good." As Rita awakens, he asks why she's there with him. She responds with perfect simplicity: "You asked me to stay, so I stayed." Growing more excited and even hopeful, Phil goes to the window and looks outside on a different street scene. A soft cover of fresh snow envelopes the town in silence. He is convinced that something new might really be happening. Returning to Rita, he makes real, openhearted contact that reveals his fragile hope. She responds with her own generosity, and they make love. Afterward, they walk out into the beautiful, snow-blanketed town of Punxsutawney. The love-filled Phil impulsively says, "Let's live here." And then wisely adds, like the transit veteran that he is, "We'll rent to start."

Chapter Eleven

GUARDIAN ANGELS AT WORK

Heart and Souls

To study the Way is to study the self. To study the self is to forget the self. To forget the self is to be enlightened by all things of the universe. To be enlightened by all things of the universe is to cast off the body and mind of the self as well as those of others. Even the traces of enlightenment are wiped out, and life with traceless enlightenment goes on forever and ever.

—Dogen

Just when it seemed that the increasing complexities of the culture had doomed the sweet simplicity of the classic film blanc, up popped a classically structured, completely endearing film called *Heart and Souls* (1993). In San Francisco around 1960, we meet four characters as they board, by turns, a Municipal bus. All are dealing with some serious unresolved issues. Penny (Alfre Woodward), an African-American single mother, is worried about having to leave her children to go to her job as a nighttime telephone operator. Leaving them under the supervision of the neighborhood "cat lady," she tucks them in with a funny little lullaby she's made up called "Mr. Hug-A-Bug Bear." Then there is Harrison (Charles Grodin), filled with remorse over having just

allowed his stage fright to botch yet another vocal audition, and Milo
(Tom Sizemore), a petty thief who has just bungled a rare attempt to
do a good deed and return a valuable stamp collection he has stolen
from a kid on behalf of his criminal boss. Last is Julia (Kyra Sedgwick),
on her way to Vallejo to tell her boyfriend that she regrets her chronic
hesitation and wants to commit to marrying him.

Unsurprisingly, the bus never reaches its destination. The driver, Hal
(David Paymer), is distracted by the sexy goings-on in a neighboring
car and doesn't see another car carrying Frank and Eva Reilly, a young
couple rushing to the hospital to have their first baby. Trying to avoid
hitting their car, Hal loses control of the bus, crashes through a guardrail,
and plunges onto Stockton Street below, killing himself and his four
passengers. At this same instant, Eva gives birth in the car to her son,
Thomas.

Because their deaths and his birth occurred simultaneously, the
ghosts of Penny, Harrison, Milo, and Julia are bound up with Thomas
by some ghostly transit logic. Thomas begins to grow up, always
surrounded by the four loving friends only he can see. At first, his
insistence on the reality of his companions is dismissed as the normal
childhood phenomenon of imaginary friends. However, by the time he
reaches seven, people are starting to worry. His parents and his teachers
even talk of sending him to a shrink. At this point, his ghostly friends
make the agonizing decision to make themselves invisible to Thomas
so he will fit in, will have a "normal childhood." Each says a painful
goodbye to the boy, leaving him sobbing and begging, "Don't leave me!"

Twenty-five years later we encounter Thomas again, now as an
adult (Robert Downey Jr.). The four ghosts are still with him, but he can
no longer sense their presence. The child who was abandoned by his
friends is now, unsurprisingly, a narcissistic man who cares for nothing
except money, possessions, and success (welcome to the '90s!). He has a
lovely girlfriend, Anne (Elisabeth Shue), but can't commit, not even to

meeting her parents. His friends' sacrifice seems to have been in vain. Thomas is certainly normal, if "normal" means vain, selfish, and living in a flatland devoid of spiritual dimension, subscribing only to material values.

But strangely, that same Muni bus reappears. (Knowing the chaotic nature of San Francisco Muni bus service, this is perhaps not as surprising as it may seem.) The driver, Hal, has assumed a transit function as a conveyor of souls to their ultimate destination. He is astonished to find out that nobody has ever told the four spirits that their task was to complete their unfinished earthly business so they could go on to heaven, and that their "corporeal being" (Thomas) was their vehicle for doing just that. The ghosts are thrilled to have some comprehension, finally, and a sense of mission. Thomas, however, is appalled. He can't believe his childhood "friends" have reappeared. Conforming to social norms, he had dismissed his childhood experiences as being at best a dream, at worst a sign of insanity. However, the abundant love and familiarity of his again-visible friends (along with some confirmation from a real psychotic that she sees them too, in vivid detail) gradually convinces him of their reality. Eventually he agrees to help them, even to let them use his body to accomplish their aims. At this point, Thomas has entered the transit world, along with his friends. He has left the familiar world of materialism and self-service and set out once again on the path of love and true seeing.

First up is Milo, who wants to return the stolen stamps. But he has to retrieve the stamps from his former boss, a thoroughgoing bad guy. Milo merges with Thomas's body so he can break into the boss's house to retrieve the stamps. The scene that follows show Downey's skills as a physical comic at their best as he runs across rooftops, hangs from ledges, and falls off onto the ground in true Buster Keaton fashion. Having retrieved the stamps, he delivers them anonymously to their real owner, now a middle-aged man living in a modest apartment with his family. Mission accomplished! And the bus appears to pick up Milo, who has now completed his life mission and is happy to go on, though sad to leave his longtime companions.

Next it is Harrison's turn. His paralyzing stage fright has kept him from ever fulfilling his gift as a singer. To help Harrison with this one, Thomas and his remaining friends need to get more creative and clever. Thomas and Penny, working with the same body, worm their way into a B. B. King concert and onto the stage. As he approaches the microphone, Thomas has a brilliant improvisational moment and commands everyone to rise for the national anthem. He turns back to Harrison and not only allows, but insists that Harrison come into his body, confront his lifetime of cowardice, stand up, and sing. We see Thomas's love and altruism growing. He knows with absolute clarity what Harrison, his real friend, needs to do, and he is not only willing, but absolutely insistent on getting him what he needs. At last, Harrison steps into Thomas's body and belts out a fervent rendition of the national anthem, singing so wonderfully that even B. B. King and his band can't resist joining in. And once again Hal and the bus materialize, and Harrison happily gets on. Another mission completed.

Thomas is beginning to act out of love. But it costs him: he was scheduled to attend that very concert with Anne and her parents. He knows she will see his presence onstage as another betrayal, and rightly so. His adored Mercedes is getting more and more banged up as Thomas strives to help his friends. The people in his firm think he's crazy. Nevertheless, he knows now what his dharma, his duty, is, and he is more and more willing to pay the personal price to help his friends fulfill their dharmas. He begins to sense that his life is not just for himself, that he exists not only as and for himself, but also as and for others, who have never been ultimately separate from him.

For all her ghostly life, Penny has been seeking reconnection with her beloved children. But to do that turns out to be not so easy. A good deal of sleuthing fails to turn up records of three orphaned kids. Eventually, the trail leads them to the old neighborhood cat lady, who reveals to Penny (in Thomas's body) that her daughters were adopted by a family in Sacramento, but that her son Billy had been swallowed up in the foster-care system, and she has no idea of his whereabouts. Despite their disappointment at the loss of Billy, Thomas, Penny, and Julia go banging off toward Sacramento, literally banging into a police car that just happens to be driven by the cop (Wren T. Brown) who had brought Thomas in for questioning after he crashed the concert. And the cop just happens to be accompanied by his wife and darling daughter. (Isn't the bardo world grand? So stereotypical and coincidental, with frequent showers of blessings!) As Thomas and the officer argue over blame for the collision, the little girl begins to cry. The policeman, who we know is Billy, holds her close and comforts her by singing "Hug-a-Bug Bear," the song that carried his mother's love and comfort with him all these years. Penny realizes that a benevolent fate has brought her boy back to her, and a grandbaby to boot. Thomas questions the officer into realizing who he really is and brings him the message of his mother's enduring love. Her heart overflowing, Penny asks to use Thomas's body for only a moment, to hug her boy one last time. The body language and look on Billy's face as Thomas embraces him pay tribute to both Downey's and Brown's consummate skill at physical comedy. Penny, in Thomas, tells Billy how he can find his sisters. Again the bus appears, and Penny joyously gets on. Julia, Thomas, and his battered Mercedes are off to Vallejo.

Through each episode we see Thomas evolving morally and spiritually. With Milo, all he needs to do is to passively allow himself to be used for the good. With Harrison, ingenuity, self-sacrifice, and tough love are needed, not just passive participation. By the time we get to Penny, we feel Thomas's total commitment. He has taken Penny's need as his own and directs his whole self—body, mind, and spirit—to her fulfillment, holding nothing back. No matter if he loses his car, if he gets arrested, loses his job or his girlfriend, no matter if everyone thinks he's gone nuts. He has become the transit hero, who knows what must be done and is willing to sacrifice himself to do it. As Pema Chödrön might say, he's becoming a baby bodhisattva, a being possessing a fundamental orientation toward the welfare of all others, who are known to be not other than the self.

So now—Julia. The two remaining travelers pull up in front of her boyfriend's home. She knows she needs to communicate both her love and her enduring regret to him, but she soon discovers that he died, alone, some years before. Thomas is crushed, filled with fear that he and Julia have failed, that the universe is not kind and just after all. But after a moment, Julia turns and smiles at him, filled with light and joy. She has recognized that her unfinished task was not, in fact, for herself, but for her beloved friend. She had to show him the karma of living without commitment, without wholeheartedness. The fulfilled karma of Julia's life is transformed into wisdom for Thomas, the last gift he needs for being a man with heart and soul.

And once again our transit hero is reborn, into the same body, the same life he had before, but with a transformed understanding and a heart broken open by caring. Thomas returns to Anne and literally offers her the keys to his loving heart. It is a lovely and charming tale, told again and again in film blanc[1] and in transit films—that life and death are not really different, that each life is a destiny to be worked out, that love conquers even death, and that once your work is done, you can let go of your life with ease and willingness and pass effortlessly beyond both life and death into everlasting union. These films say that life and death are ultimately fair, that the laws of karma are immutable, but also that grace is unfailing. Death is not to be feared, because the self is eternal. A pretty story indeed! No wonder we love to see and hear it again and again, our very own "Hug-a-Bug Bear" song.

Chapter Twelve

SYMPATHY FOR THE DEVIL

Interview with the Vampire

There are two kinds of suffering: the suffering that leads to more suffering and the suffering that leads to the end of suffering. If you are not willing to face the second kind of suffering, you will surely continue to experience the first.

—Achaan Chah

Vampires have always been popular, but these days they are everywhere, from the HBO series *True Blood* to the blockbuster *Twilight* movies. Why vampires? Why now? There are a number of blood trails we could follow.

Of course, nowadays common perception is that the vampires are the 1 percent—the bankers, the corporations, and the politicians they have bought, who are sucking the body politic dry; the obscenely rich preying upon the less fortunate with promises of eternal youth, prosperity, and well-being. The Coca-Cola Company encourages us to "open happiness" in a bottle of chemicals and sugary water. These predators encourage us to believe that the acquisition of celebrity and riches is available to any of us and that with enough fame and money we can banish sorrow and live forever. We surrender to their seduction, turn away from the light of reality, and embrace the bloodsuckers, capitalism, and consumerism. Our life energy is drained from us. We exist as mere material beings, devoid of soul, and the 1 percent grow warm with our lifeblood.[1]

From a psychological viewpoint, the vampire symbolizes the malignant narcissism that pervades our culture, the sense of vast entitlement that allows us to devour both the planet and the labor of impoverished millions, the endless, insatiable hunger for *more*. For the narcissist, the world and other beings are only a mirror in which one longs to see oneself reflected. If the reflection looks good, it is a good mirror; if not, smash it to bits. Nobody ever says, "So, Mirror, how was your day?" The mirror's only function is to reflect. Part of the hell of vampires is their inability to see themselves reflected in a mirror. Lacking that reflection, they are monsters for whom other creatures have no value, except to satisfy their craving.

As a religious image, the vampire is an inverted Christ. Unlike the one who willingly offered up his body and his blood for the salvation of all, vampires take the blood, the life essence, for their own satisfaction. Vampires are a perfect image of the demonic, of pure metaphysical evil. Theirs is the innate sinfulness of the unredeemed ego, putting its own selfish and insatiable demands in place of the law of God, which commands that we do not kill. Vampires are condemned to live in darkness, cut off from the holy light, compelled by their nature to sin.

We recognize the vampire in our narcissism, our greed, our bottomless hunger. But we also recognize in ourselves the vampire's victim, that deep desire to surrender the burden of responsibility and swoon into the arms of beautiful oblivion. And vampires' seduction is that they speak to that within us which longs to be wanted totally, to be irresistible, and to be relieved finally of the pain that comes with conscious life. Something in us longs to be consumed in ecstatic union, like an orgasm that never ends. We find our separateness so unsatisfactory that we will buy transcendence of self in almost any form, including, or especially, oblivion.

Such a vat of powerful emotions would seem the, well, lifeblood of a dynamically engrossing motion picture. Alas, despite its roster of stars, its lavish production values, and Tom Cruise's manic performance as the vampire Lestat, Anne Rice's screenplay for *Interview with the Vampire: The Vampire Chronicles* (1994) has a curiously flat quality. It suffers, as well, from Brad Pitt's performance as Louis; he needed to convey a profound ennui, but ended up sounding merely flat. Nevertheless, we think the movie offers a unique existential view of the vampire dilemma. The director, Neil Jordan, has said that "these are the saddest vampires you've ever seen." That is saying quite a lot, since vampire movies nearly always convey a sense of the tragedy of being damned, cut off from the holy light. But in this movie, one vampire, Louis, is indeed the saddest of them all.

Louis de Pointe du Lac became a vampire in Louisiana in 1791. His wife and child had died in childbirth, and he was lost in grief. He longed for death, invited it, and the invitation was accepted by the vampire Lestat. Lestat gives Louis a choice—to accept death at his hands (or more precisely, his fangs) or to become a vampire himself. Lestat offers the grieving Louis exactly what the separate self most desperately wants when he promises him, "Sickness and death can never touch you again." He can go on, changeless in an ever-changing world, free from the suffering that inheres in human life.

In this moment, Louis refuses to accept that suffering. He denies the First Noble Truth taught by the Buddha: life contains suffering. This truth is nothing personal, though we take it as a personal failure or affront. To love is to accept the preordained loss. Either I will see my beloved die or my beloved will see me die. That's the deal. Good times are wonderful, but they simply don't last. The unlasting reality of everything and the unpredictability of life are painful in themselves. To imagine you can be exempt from suffering is the purest narcissism, the insistence that life conform to my terms rather than my conforming to its. This truth is noble because it calls us to recognize our actual situation: that we are not in control.

But Lestat is right about Louis: when it comes right down to it, Louis chooses vampirism over true death. He accepts Lestat's offer, quite consciously lives through his last sunrise, and says goodbye to the light. He receives the vampiric communion of blood and is changed forever. At first he is charmed by the beautiful night world revealed to his heightened senses, but he quickly realizes the terrible price he has paid for immortal life. He must live on the blood of others, kill to survive. Louis has now become a bardo being, neither alive nor dead, wandering through time and space trying to find out who he is, where he comes from, what his existence is for. His nature is to be a predator, yet killing fills him with guilt. Lestat has no time for Louis's guilt. His narcissism is perfect. His nature is to kill, and he glories in killing. For him, killing is the most profoundly erotic act, the ultimate expression of himself. He prefers the blood of evildoers, simply because it tastes better and they are easier to catch. For Lestat, Louis's scruples are absurd. To be a vampire is to kill, and killing is glorious, the ultimate power. For Lestat, killing is celebration.

But in Louis's transit world, unending life in unending darkness has no meaning, and he is still somehow human enough to need meaning. He needs to understand his existence, this undeath bought at the nightly price of murder. He is overwhelmed by the pain of being both a killer and an ethical being, in some way capable, and needful, of love. And it is that need that Lestat preys upon, getting Louis to collude with him in an incredibly monstrous act: the creation of Claudia (Kirsten Dunst), a child vampire, in order to have the solace of companionship. Out of the monstrous couplehood of Lestat and Louis, they create a demonic child, deprive her of life and of change, and make her forever both a helpless child and a ruthless killer. They create her as a companion for Louis, and she bonds with him immediately. He has bought himself a love object at a price of previously unimaginable evil because he could not bear his own suffering, the pain of his loneliness. Lestat saw that weakness in Louis and seduced him into deeper darkness.

And for a while the devil's bargain works. The three travel the world as a predatory family. Their doll-child is beautiful and adoring, dressed in beautiful clothes made at night; she learns to play the piano (and only in a naughty moment fails to heed the "no killing in the house" rule). Eventually, however, Claudia begins to realize the horror of her situation, the perpetual helplessness and immaturity inflicted on her. She turns on Lestat and forms a demonic alliance with Louis, and together they seemingly murder Lestat. Louis and Claudia travel to Europe, seeking to understand vampire nature and culture. Louis is literally looking for his ancestors, to understand who and what he is. It's as though they are wandering through countries and epochs (wandering is a sure sign that you are in the transit state) looking for others like them, a tribe to which they could belong, and most of all, looking for a teacher, someone who can disclose the mystery of their vampire existence.

And more and more Claudia feels the horror of never growing up, never being able to live independently, never being strong enough to make vampire companions for herself. She needs a caretaker, and she feels Louis being pulled away by his searching. Claudia finds a perfect candidate, a young woman who needs a child who can never die to replace the one she lost. They both demand that Louis make the woman a vampire mother for Claudia. And, again, Louis is unable to resist being drawn deeper into horror. He drains her blood and gives her his. He makes a vampire. In this moment he plunges into the depths of his own hell: the making of Claudia inevitably gave rise to this consequence. Unable to bear his own loneliness, he allowed a helpless companion to be made for him. Eventually the companion needed a companion, and the wheel of karma continued to turn. Yet even this new circumstance does not save Claudia and her "mother." They are imprisoned in a dungeon where they are burned up by the sunlight. Louis has lost his only beloved, his only companion, his only child. So here in his deathless existence, death and loss have come again. The thing he gave his soul never to experience again, death, has found him again in his transit.

Everything is ashes. Louis is thrown into pure remorse. He has given his soul to evil, and it has bought him nothing—no permanence, no security, no peace. He has only an eternity of regret. It is from this remorse that another vampire, Armand, promises to save Louis. He introduces him to the *Theatre des Vampyrs* and a vampire tribe. But the theatrics are emptier than empty, and Armand has no real knowledge or salvation to bestow. What he has to teach is how to live without regret. Louis refuses that teaching, saying, "What if all I have is my suffering, my regret?" He is, at last, willing to accept the suffering that leads to the end of suffering, choosing the conscious suffering of his remorse over the promise of relief. He knows that he is depraved, a killer by nature. As he continues to kill, his guilt is absurd. As Lestat says, "Merciful death! Spare me your precious guilt!" Louis also knows that he is moral by nature, that indeed the last scrap of his human nature did not in fact die in the room where he made Claudia her vampire-mother. He is a vampire: he loves, and he kills. This is his fate, and he finally accepts it, not from any hope of redemption, but simply because there is finally nothing else left to do. He tried to escape suffering, but he brought his mind with him, no matter where he went, whether he ate rats or humans, whether he felt guilty or not. Trying to escape his own suffering, he brought pain and death to others, even to the one he loved most. Trying to escape death, he found an endless transit state, wandering, in need of redemption and disqualified from grace, unable either to live or to die.

Louis's truth is this: he kills; he mourns his lost love. He is at last willing just to exist in the face of two absolute truths. He must kill to exist, and killing is wrong. He contains within himself these irreconcilable truths. They rub against each other constantly, becoming a burning within, from which there is no escape. And Louis no longer seeks escape. He knows himself to be alone, and he accepts that. He knows himself damned, beyond hope of change. The old Buddhist masters might say that here is where the path begins. Only when all our strategies, all our demonic bargains have failed are we finally willing to face ourselves and what we have brought about in our doomed quest for a permanent, eternal, happy sense of separate self. We have sucked the life out of others and been sucked dry ourselves. We are helpless to be other than we are, vampires, and yet we have a built-in tropism toward the light, an aspiration toward the good, a sense of eternity. That's all we know. And in his acceptance of his fate comes a bit of grace: the movies. Here, he can once again see the beautiful dawn, first in silver, then later in glorious color. He can once again vicariously experience the light of day, if only as a reflection off a silver screen.

So one night Louis tells his story in a room on Divisadero Street in San Francisco, trying, perhaps, to communicate the pain of living in the pressure of the inherent contradiction, knowing oneself to be an evil being and yet trying to do a good act by telling this tale, which we have just watched as a movie. Louis is walking the path of conscious suffering—unable to stop sinning and yet unwilling to still the consciousness of sin. His sense of separate selfhood is a sense of total alienation, and yet he knows the indelible memory of having loved and been loved, though by a demonic child. He knows himself most deeply as the one who loved and still mourns. His remorse, his mourning, and the death that cannot be his are the only teachers Louis has. He at last bows to his teachers, and as he accepts the burden of his suffering, his hell transforms into a purgatory.

He hopes only to tell his story, as a profoundly cautionary tale. But the recipient of his tale, an interviewer named Malloy (Christian Slater), can hear only the wild energy and apparent freedom in Louis's story, and he begs to be made a vampire. The glamour of evil is undiminished by the bitterness of experience. Louis is filled with rage and tosses the terrified interviewer out into the night. Crossing the Golden Gate Bridge in his convertible, Malloy begins to listen to his tapes of Louis's story, and, lo, up pops the irrepressible Lestat, who, after introducing himself to Malloy with "I assume I need no introduction," sinks his teeth into Malloy's neck. When he hears Louis's voice on the tape, he moans wearily, "Louis, Louis, still whining. I've had to listen to that for centuries." Sweeping up the quivering Malloy, he goes on, "Don't be afraid, I'm going to give you the choice I never had."

The night is dark and the bridge lights are golden. We listen to the car radio as the Rolling Stones demand some "Sympathy for the Devil." And, like Lestat's next victim, we are seduced again. And the beat goes on, and the beat goes on, as the wheels of karma turn.

Chapter Thirteen

DE PROFUNDIS

The Sixth Sense

We who think of ourselves as the living could really be called the dead. We are the unawakened, living our lives in a dream—a dream that will continue after death, then through life after life, until we truly awaken.

—Francesca Fremantle

But why, you may ask, would it be necessary to tell someone he or she is dead? If any ghost or spirit were still around, wouldn't it know that salient fact—that it is dead? Isn't death a marked-in-time event, like birth? Wouldn't I know if I were dead, just as I know I'm awake right now?

Well, maybe not. If we examine our experience a bit more closely, we notice that states of consciousness slide around quite a lot. Haven't you ever had a memory and not been sure whether you dreamed it or it really happened? Like the familiar story of the monk Chuang Tzu, who fell asleep and dreamed he was a butterfly: when he awoke, he wondered whether he was indeed Chuang Tzu dreaming he was a butterfly or a butterfly dreaming he was Chuang Tzu. Trance states are a familiar part of everyday life, as anyone who has ridden the subway or been on a long car ride knows. In the hypnagogic state between waking and falling asleep, one can even catch glimpses of realms other than this material one. Indeed, wisdom traditions tell us that what we take to be our waking state is in fact a state of sleep, in which we concoct a dream world out of social conditioning, unreliable memories, residues of past experiences, imitation, appropriation, negative emotions, and unquestioned assumptions.

Movies, of course, are another state of uncertainty. On one hand, we know that what we are seeing, hearing, and feeling is unreal, a mere play of light projected through a moving strip of sprocket-edged celluloid or, in these days, more likely high-definition video. On the other hand, we respond to these images with deep feeling, empathic involvement, and corresponding shifts in our brain and body chemistry, often more than we do to actual people and situations in our outside-the-theater lives. Often large segments of our inner life are devoted to fantasy involvements with film characters or movie stars; stalkers are only the most extreme form of this behavior. During the writing of this book, a story broke that some major Hollywood players were seeking to feature the stars of the past in new movies by utilizing computer technology to re-create the no-longer-with-us performers—and Elvis still lives at Graceland. We see someone die in one film and be reborn as someone else in a different movie. Reality, it seems, is not as solid and linear as it's cracked up to be.

It is not far-fetched to imagine that some individuals could be unaware they have died. They seem to be in the same or a similar body; they continue to think and act in a largely familiar world, even if it's shot through with peculiar coincidences and unsettling shifts of time and space. So in the Tibetan bardo ceremony the first information given, with compassion, to the dead person is, "Now you are dead. You can't come back to this body." It is sad but true: until we can know our true state, our true situation, we have no possibility of orienting ourselves or dealing with what is unfolding.

This confusion is what confronts Malcolm, a dedicated child psychologist, played by Bruce Willis in M. Night Shyamalan's blockbuster film *The Sixth Sense* (1999). At the start of the movie, we see Malcolm as a sweet, funny, devoted guy who "sounds like Dr. Seuss when he's drunk." He loves both his work with troubled kids and Anna, his adoring wife, though sometimes those two priorities conflict. He has just been honored by the city of Philadelphia with a plaque. (This award is a pretty good sign one's career is over, right up there with a gold watch acknowledging you as a good servant of the status quo, a holder of the received wisdom.) Quite rightly, Malcolm knows that the only really valuable thing about the plaque is its frame. Nevertheless, the plaque lets us know right away that Malcolm is meant to be a hero. His strongest desire is to help. Then, in a moment, a tender scene with his wife turns threatening; we see him confronted by a former child patient, Vincent Gray, who feels utterly betrayed by him and has broken into his house. Malcolm is scared, and he doesn't really understand what's going on, but he uses all his available social and professional skills to defuse the situation. First he tells Vincent that he has broken into a private residence at 47 Locust Street and that there are no needles or prescription drugs. Then he tells Vincent he remembers him as "very, very compassionate." But Vincent is way past responding to these ordinary maneuvers; in fact, they convince him all over again that Malcolm doesn't understand him in the least. In his despair, Vincent suddenly shoots Malcolm and then himself. In a sudden shift of perspective to an overhead camera, we see Malcolm falling back onto the bed.

The scene shifts to the following autumn. We find Malcolm studying a file, and as he looks up a boy emerges from the building next door, while at the same time the camera closes in on the boy's name on the file. As if magically, the file slowly fades, changing from "Vincent Gray, age 10, parents divorced, extremely anxious, possible mood disorder" to "Cole Sear, age 10, parents divorced, etc." This metamorphosis is the first sign that we may have entered the transit realm. We see Cole (Haley Joel Osment) running through the streets; from his gait, we can see how anxious and inhibited he is, and how afraid. He runs into a Catholic church, where he crouches on a kneeler surrounded by his toy soldiers and begins to pray in Latin: "De profundis, clamo ad te, domine." He is a soul in the profundity of torment, crying out from the depths for help from beyond. And Malcolm shows up in the church. He sits down with Cole, noting that they had an appointment earlier in the day, but that he, Malcolm, has missed it. He acknowledges that he is having trouble keeping track of time. Malcolm knows he is haunted by his failure with Vincent; he is desperate to succeed in helping Cole. He has such a good heart and a sincere sympathy for Cole, but all he can bring forth are his conventional understandings of psychology. Malcolm appears to have a theory all worked out, just as he did with Vincent: that Cole's problems are connected with his parents' divorce. If only!

Malcolm is about to discover there are indeed more things in heaven and earth than are dreamed of in his psychology—and that causes are much more complex than that psychology allows. It is not that Cole isn't marked by the divorce or that he is not trying to use magical talismans like his father's glasses and watch to try to maintain a sense of his presence. It's just that Cole's problems go far beyond those realms. In this way, conventional psychology, with its focus on the diagnostic categories, brain chemistry, and treatment plans in the *Diagnostic and Statistical Manual of Mental Disorders*, misses all the extraordinary dimensions of life. It situates us in a flatland of material objects and conditioned mental processes. It supports a world in which the intrusion of transpersonal material into ordinary consciousness is considered mental disease and is treated with drugs and therapy in order to force the sufferer back into the flatland of social agreements, commonly called sanity.

So Malcolm tries his professional moves on Cole. Some of these moves are creative and skillful indeed, like the mind-reading game. However, Malcolm's assumptions quickly prove wrong and only succeed in convincing Cole that he, though a nice man, can't really help him. And he is right. Because Cole's real problem is that he sees dead people. In fact, as we see from the photos on his mother's wall, he has seen them all his life. Even in infancy, he had a look of terror. Imagine—being a child and seeing and hearing dead and tormented souls everywhere. Every moment is filled with terror, and you bear that burden alone. Anyone who gets even a whiff of the anxiety that pervades your life is repelled and calls you freak.

Cole's only solace is his mother, Lynn (Toni Collette), a youngish woman, attractive, with striking auburn hair, dramatic makeup, and colorfully varnished nails. Although she is bewildered and afraid for her boy, she loves him wholeheartedly and refuses ever to think of him as a freak. Here again is the Good Mother, the Good Goddess, the Beatrice whose love brings the soul out of hell. Without her steadiness, Cole would have gone under, perhaps descended into the childhood schizophrenia Malcolm is so ready to suppose for him. However, protecting her goodness from the true horror of his life has become Cole's mission. Performing his mission costs him dearly in loneliness. When he drew a picture in school of a man with a knife stuck in his neck, the school called a meeting; his mother cried. Now Cole doesn't draw his reality any more; he draws "people smiling, dogs running, rainbows. Nobody calls a meeting about rainbows." In his will to protect his beloved mother, Cole shows himself to be another hero in training, devoted to others' good.

So these two suffering beings, these would-be heroes, encounter each other. Though Malcolm tries to be the therapist, it is Cole who asks Malcolm the crucial questions: "Are you good at what you do?" Malcolm replies, "I used to be." Cole asks, "Why are you so sad?" At first Malcolm tries to deflect the question, then takes a breath and tells the truth, about his catastrophic failure with Vincent and his alienation from his wife. Moved by Malcolm's honesty, Cole dares to tell his secret: "I see dead people." Despite his promises not to reveal the boy's secret, in the very next scene we see Malcolm dictating into his recorder, giving his ignorant assessment of Cole's condition.

Nevertheless, Cole and Malcolm are forming a bond, which persists, even in the face of Malcolm's limitations and Cole's terrible isolation. Their growing love for and trust in each other becomes the most important thing for both of them, and it allows them to persist in their attempts to communicate, despite their painful misattunements. One evening, Malcolm listens to an old tape recording of a session with Vincent; turning up the volume, he hears a strange, disembodied voice saying, "Yo no quiero morir" (I don't want to die). At last, his world cracks open, and he understands both Vincent and Cole, and the overwhelming terror they endure.

Now it is Malcolm who can ask the right question: "What do the ghosts want?" He and Cole together realize that what they want is help—the very thing that both Cole and Malcolm have always wanted to give to someone. This realization is the empowering moment for Cole—and for Malcolm, who becomes the healer he has always wanted to be. He gives Cole the courage and the sense of purpose to transform his curse into a gift. Rather than trying to reduce Cole to some pathology, he inspires him to integrate all of his experience into his heroic project. He transmits his own gift of meeting and understanding into Cole; he makes Cole into the healer he has always been meant to be.

And in the process, Malcolm discovers what he wants. He wants to be able to talk to his wife the way they used to, as if there were no one else in the world.

To ask the right question, and to know what you want and need—these are the two great things. So again we see the formation of a hero—someone who knows what needs to be done and is willing to do it. Malcolm has transcended the limits of his comprehension of life and is now able to accompany Cole fully as the boy undergoes his own initiatory ordeal.

Armed with his new mission, Cole is able to ask the right question the next time Cole sees a ghost, a vomiting girl: "What do you want?" Despite his fear and revulsion, his courage prevails. In the next scene, Cole and Malcolm are on a bus, heading for the ghostly girl's funeral. Once again the girl shows up, and she leads Cole to a video tape. (This theme of an object that passes between two worlds is a common one in transit films: for example, the penny in *Ghost*.) He, in turn, gives the tape to the girl's father. It shows the girl's mother poisoning her food. Cole's heroic action saves the dead girl's sister from being another victim of the mother's psychopathic condition. Sitting beside her on a swing, Cole gives the sister one of the dead girl's favorite puppets, and he answers her question honestly by telling her that her sister won't be coming back again. Cole has freed the dead girl, and freed himself and Malcolm too.

And now we see Cole transformed into the school play's Young Arthur, who by his purity of heart (always Cole's best quality) pulls the sword from the stone. As we see him playfully thrusting his sword before the stained glass windows, we know he has become the holy warrior who crosses all dimensions to free beings from their suffering and help them on their way to the light. His whole being is transformed by having found his mission. Malcolm too has completed his holy and heroic task. He has reached into the impenetrable darkness and freed a tortured child. He has balanced the karmic scales, Cole for Vincent. He has become the hero, the healer, the father he always wanted to be. He found in himself, not the right answers, but the right questions.[1] And, of course, his basic goodness, his love has brought him through. At the crucial time, he cared more for Cole than for his ideas; he allowed his conceptions to be turned upside down for love of this boy and for his own desire to make things right.

Maybe it always comes down to this: what do we love more than our minds, more than our safety, more than understanding or being right? For most of us, it is probably the people we love. For some of our transit heroes, it is truth or harmony, putting things right. For others, it is love of all and everything. For Malcolm and Cole, it is love, yes, but also service. Both of them find meaning for their lives only in opening themselves to others in order to free them from their suffering, no matter what the danger or risk. In this opening is their heroism. In opening, they imitate Christ; they become Christ for each other. From the depths of their pain, both cry out for redemption. And redemption is what each one gets. Cole doesn't get what he wanted—the ghosts don't go away—but through his willingness to minister to them, to support them on their journey, he becomes a savior. Malcolm, too, doesn't get what he wanted, exactly. But he gets what he needs: to heal his failure with Vincent and to really help a child. Cole, in his boyish mercy, gives Malcolm the secret wisdom: he can talk to his beloved wife in a different realm, the realm of sleep (another bardo), and she can hear him.

Cole acknowledges that he won't see Malcolm again; their work together is complete. But he suggests that they pretend they'll see each other tomorrow, and Malcolm agrees, just for pretend. But Malcolm and Cole have come through many dimensions together; both of them sense that separation is only apparent, not real. Cole and Malcolm now both go to make peace with their beloveds, with the Divine Feminine herself.

Cole and his mother, Lynn, are stuck in a traffic jam; there's been an accident up ahead. Cole bravely announces to his mother that he is now ready to communicate, to tell his secret. "I see ghosts." Lynn is overwhelmed with dismay and fear for her little boy. The familiar paralyzing anxiety about upsetting her passes swiftly across Cole's face. Yet the young hero persists. He tells her that Lynn's deceased mother, his grandmother, often comes to visit him. He conveys Grandma's message that she secretly watched Lynn's dance recital from the wings and that the answer to Lynn's question ("Do I make you proud?") is "Every day!" The child has healed the mother; they hug each other in a flooding of love and relief.

Now Malcolm's journey can be fulfilled. He can be of help, and he can express his love. The worlds of life and death, waking and sleeping, illusion and reality merge and are revealed as always and only one. Malcolm walks into his house and begins talking to his sleeping wife, telling her of his love, that she was never second to his work, that she was always first, first without a second. As she stirs, he sees his wedding ring drop from her hand onto the flour. To his shock, Malcolm looks at his hand and sees that the ring is gone. Standing on the stairs in a panic, he begins to recall the shooting. His shirt is again covered with blood, and he feels himself lying on the bed, now feeling strangely at peace. He tells Anna, "I think it's going to be all right. I don't feel any pain now." And he dies, but not before telling the sleeping Anna, "I think I can go now. Sleep now, and tomorrow everything will be different." Leaving Anna to live her own life, Malcolm is free to leave the realm of the living.

Malcolm—and we as well—just lived this whole transit experience together, all contained in the moments of his dying.[2] Time and space have proved as elusive as we suspected, and the situation was not as we thought. Months of events took place in the blink of an eye. One boy became another boy, and that boy was healed. In healing another, Malcolm himself was healed, and he passed the healing mission on to Cole, who has learned to live with the ghosts that are part of his life. Malcolm has become what he has always wanted to be: an instrument of God's peace. His life and death are complete.

Apparently it works this way: each soul cries out from the depths to the Divine, and the Divine responds, not usually with an angel or a saint, not with a chariot of fire, but with another pain-wracked being just as lost and confused as ourselves, only different. That being's suffering touches our hearts, and we would do anything to relieve it. That willingness leads us beyond our concepts of who we are and of what we can do, until we finally transcend ourselves. It is then that we discover the wisdom of the Prayer of St. Francis:

> For it is in giving that we receive,
> It is in pardoning that we are pardoned,
> And it is in dying that we are born to eternal life.

It seems that we are meant to be Christ for each other—to find ourselves by losing ourselves out of love for another and for the truth. No chariot of fire is coming from the sky to save us—we seem to be here to do it for ourselves and for each other. Christ, after all, was fully a human—he was born like us, lived with us, ate with us, and died like us. That's why he is called the Son of Man. His divinity and his humanity are one. And when we allow ourselves to accept that miracle, ours are too. Amen.

Chapter Fourteen

SHORT TAKES

Purgatory, The Others, Passengers, and a Bit of Empty Luminosity

Although sages report
the nature of awareness to be luminosity,
this limitless radiance cannot be contained
within any language or sacramental system.
Although the very essence of Mind
is to be void of either subjects or objects,
It tenderly embraces all life within its womb.

—Tilopa's Song to Naropa

As we saw in *The Sixth Sense*, not knowing when you have entered the transit state can be confusing at best and often very frightening. Why is it so difficult, and necessary, to realize you are dead? Conventional Buddhist wisdom—and Buddhists have had long over two thousand years to work on this topic—tells us that the bardo/transit state, like waking, dreaming, dreamless sleep, and the states caused by hypnosis and psychedelic drugs, is simply another state of consciousness. Just as the dream state can seem so real that we can confuse it with the waking state or be terrified by nightmares, so the transit state seems not unlike dreaming or waking life. However, it is imperative that the self recognize the actual state in order to orient and respond to the experiences that appear to be unfolding. Without accurate understanding of one's true state, there is no way to proceed toward a favorable outcome.

So, the next few movies are about problems that can arise when you don't know you are dead, or perhaps you are alive but find yourself hanging out with dead people. In other words, they deal with recognizing alternative states of conscious being. Which takes us to *Purgatory*, where (according to the DVD jacket blurb), "Cowboy legend meets the supernatural . . . an eerie saga that's west of the Pecos . . . and south of eternity."

It was inevitable, we guess, but in 1999 a guy named Uli Edel made a not-half-bad shoot-'em-up western/transit crossover movie called *Purgatory*. It's about an ornery outlaw gang led by Blackjack Britton (Eric Roberts) that robs a bank and kills a woman, who dies in the arms of Sonny (Brad Rowe), the youngest member of the gang. The gang then skedaddles into the desert, pursued by a posse. Caught up in a dust storm, they enter what seems a large cave, coming out into an apparently peaceful woodland with verdant pastures situated "between somewhere and nowhere," containing a small town called Refuge. Spiritual adepts and seekers alike will immediately recognize the word, as in "taking refuge in the Buddha," an act involving the challenging chores of transforming anger into compassion, delusion into wisdom, and desire into generosity. Unfortunately, the smarmy Blackjack and his gang have other plans.

Refuge is a pleasant western town where the sheriff (Sam Shepard) and his deputy (Donnie Wahlberg) don't carry weapons. There is no jail because there is no crime. Swearing is allowed only in the saloon. Whenever there's a problem the church bells sound, and all the residents gather at the church. Dutiful citizens? Sonny is the first to notice something unusual when a stagecoach arrives carrying a passenger identical to the woman who so recently died in his arms. He also seems to think that some of the residents look familiar. Meanwhile the outlaw varmints are tearing up the town, and its residents have flocked to the church for a powwow.

Putting a number of facts together, Sonny realizes that Refuge is functioning as a kind of purgatory, where famous dead men who had lived lives of violence can gain redemption by avoiding violence and resisting the temptations they had succumbed to in life. The penalty for failure is hell, the reward for success, heaven. So who's in Refuge? Well, Wild Bill Hickok, the current sheriff, Doc Holliday, Billie the Kid, Jesse James, and a who's who of other former bad guys. Wild Bill has only twenty-four hours to go before his sentence is up; and then it's the place upstairs.

Fully aware that they cannot engage in violence, the townsfolk decide to stand and fight before they will surrender to evil, even though they may also surrender all hope of reaching heaven. Their biblical injunction is "Resist not evil" (Matthew 5:39). That, and the fact that they are understandably a little rusty, gives rise to a touch of trepidation, but these are men who seldom, if ever, have turned the other cheek. Their redemption lies in the selflessness of their decision: not doing violence on behalf of their egos or passions but for the greater good of the town and its holy function. The bad guys, who thought they could take over the town, are filled with shock and awe as they face the legends of the West. There is a classic shoot-out, and the men of Refuge triumph, but Sonny, who has sided with the town, is mortally wounded—his transit birth as a resident of Refuge.

At the edge of town sits a mist-shrouded graveyard, gated, but with no walls. In this eerie, otherworldly space, a Cerberus-like being, an ancient Indian whose task is to carry the evil dead to their fate, guards the gate. The battle over, he busies himself carrying and throwing the bodies and souls of Blackjack and his gang into the fiery pit of hell. The men of Refuge, having fought evil, fear that they too will be thrown into hell. Even as they are being led to hell's gate, a stagecoach arrives from heaven. The driver has a message: "The Creator may be tough, but He ain't blind"; they stood up to evil and will be taken to heaven. Sonny stays in Refuge, to be with the woman he loves and to take over as the new sheriff. The fully redeemed sheriff rides off in the stagecoach bathed in light as it nears heaven's gate.

Purgatory makes it clear that "refuge" can be anywhere. Alternately, taking refuge *is* a purgatory, a place where conscious suffering becomes the path to no suffering. The key to change lies in recognizing the situation we find ourselves in and, if it is one of anger, delusion, and desire, then seeking refuge from our self-deception and fears, especially our fear of death. Freedom from suffering, our awakening, comes from insight into our own reality. It is not some magical empowerment, but an act involving those exacting tasks of transforming anger into compassion, delusion into wisdom, and desire into generosity. If you ain't clear on this, Buckaroos, just ask the good citizens of Refuge.

Alejandro Amenábar's beautifully produced and skillfully executed *The Others* (2001) features a country home containing a mixed bag of multigenerational ghosts who either know or do not know they are dead, but are trying to live together. (And you thought your roommate situation was bad.) It is 1945, and the war in Europe is ending. At a remote country estate on the Isle of Jersey, Grace Stewart (Nicole Kidman) and her two children, Anne and Nicholas, live an isolated existence—the servants have run off because the place is haunted—waiting and hoping for the return of their husband/father from the war. He has been reported missing in action. The children are kept secluded in the darkened house because they are said to suffer from acute photosensitivity: in other words, they are kept in the dark.

One day two women and a man show up, saying they are seeking work as servants. The older woman, Mrs. Mills (Fionnula Flanagan), functioning as spokesperson, relates how they had worked for the previous owners, but left at the outbreak of the war, during which the Germans had occupied the island. The new servants are hired, and the arrangement works for a while; then it begins to unravel. The house does seem to be haunted by someone or something, and the children are most susceptible to its force. The father returns, but his presence is quite ambiguous. He appears to be in shell shock, delicate and ragged. His primary purpose is to say goodbye and return to the front, but the implication is that he may be dead. The unspoken truth of the situation in the house rapidly increases the tension already existing between its occupants. The servants are increasingly open about the fact that they are coequal occupiers of the house with the mother and two children.

The children attempt to run away. Someone or something removes all the heavy curtains from the house's windows, allowing in the light. These strange occurrences culminate in all parties being forced to face the preternatural reality of their situation. The servants had indeed worked there, but in the late 1890s. All three had died of tuberculosis. The mother, Grace, had murdered her children and then killed herself when the father left for war. He died in Germany. The children do not suffer from acute photosensitivity, but are victims of their mother's strategy of keeping from them the truth of what she has done.

And in a final, quite clever twist, there *are* ghosts. For the disembodied Grace, children, and servants who claim this house as home, the actual living occupants of the house are experienced as ghosts. These living beings create the same fear in the spirit occupants of the house as is felt by the living occupants when confronted by the ghostly interlopers whose story we are witnessing. We watch as the living residents conduct a séance addressing their concerns that the house is malignantly haunted. Their conjecture is confirmed, and the next scene shows the living family abandoning the residence, fearful for the health of their son, the most sensitive to the presence of the dead children. The farsighted and firm-minded Mrs. Mills acknowledges their departure to the remaining ghostly residents, warning them that others will follow, but she holds firm to her pragmatic opinion that "we must all learn to live together—the living and the dead." Indeed!

Dealing essentially with the same issue, nonrecognition of one's state of being, is a movie that kept popping up on one of the Encore channels, *Passengers* (2008). We had not heard much about it and suspected it didn't make much of a run in theaters, but it did have an intriguing tag line on the DVD case: "The line between this world and the next is about to be crossed," a promising premise. We are all, to some extent or other, dying to know what lies beyond this mortal existence. So we watched as naïve young psychologist Claire Summers (Anne Hathaway) is hired by an airline to lead a small trauma-recovery group of passengers who have survived a plane crash. Almost immediately she begins to uncover conflicting accounts of the accident. At first, she believes that shock and trauma can explain her patients' widely discordant accounts of what happened—until, that is, the eight or nine survivors begin to disappear one by one.

Eric (Patrick Wilson), a surviving passenger to whom Claire has become attracted, is determined to uncover the truth about what is becoming of his fellow trauma-group members. Was the crash due to pilot error or malfeasance on the part of the airlines? Are the disappearances the result of a cover-up to eliminate eyewitnesses to what happened on the plane? The deeper Eric and Claire delve into the ever-accumulating circumstances and the more they observe the often-bizarre behavior of the decreasing number of survivors, the closer Eric comes to the belief that he and the other survivors may indeed be dead and experiencing some type of alternate state of being. A very practical guy, he tests his theory by standing on the tracks of a swiftly approaching electric train. We see, through Claire's eyes, the train make contact with Eric, pass through him, and move on. Eric is still standing. Claire is devastated, partly because she wasn't aware of Eric's suspicions, but mostly because she has been clueless that, like everyone in her group, she is dead.

The brief remainder of the movie consists of her coming, with Eric's loving help, to the realization and acceptance of the fact that she, like the others, was a passenger on the plane and shares their fate. The film ends with the couple sailing off on beautiful Puget Sound.

Not great, but nevertheless entertaining movies, our three short takes bring up some thoughts on the luminous quality of lives lived in the transit realm. Like Mrs. Mills and her housemates, like Claire and Eric, and like the striving-to-be-better reformers of *Purgatory*, we "passengers" are reaching for the light. But so much of our ordinary, day-to-day existence is spent in the belief that we know what reality is and what state of consciousness we are in—whether we are dead or alive, awake, dreaming, or somewhere in between. For many of us there are times when we are not quite sure. We have certain memories that we can't quite place as dreams, actual experience, or, who knows, some past life's fragments floating up from the depths of our consciousness. The truth of the matter is that we are often confused about what state we are in. We fluctuate like the proverbial Chuang Tzu, who upon waking wonders whether he has been dreaming he is a butterfly or whether he is a butterfly now dreaming he is Chuang Tzu. Perennial wisdom tells us that even when we think that we are awake and that what we are experiencing is real, we are actually in a kind of trance or dream state, confronting concocted images and constructing the condition we call reality. Given our confusion about the waking state, it is not so surprising that we can be confused at death, when it is said that all our differing states become a kind of sliding, intermeshing reality.

In its own inimitable way, Hollywood keeps showing us certain truths about this reality. Of course, not in the way Hollywood would like us to believe—it's not that its stories are more true or false, fair or biased, inclusive or exclusionary, or any of those other things critics point out, but that a movie is an experience with a beginning, middle, and end, after which we leave and return to our customary reality. What films show us is that, whatever the storyline, director, characters, and scripts, they are always just movies—compelling, involving, real, yet unreal—mere projections of light conforming to the conditioned structures of our minds: an empty luminosity. We witness this seductive display of energy and movement in all its beauty and horror, but because the spectacle is so vividly realistic and because it conforms to our own conditioned structures, we all too quickly forget that what we are watching is not ultimately real, but rather a set of interpretations projected through the lens of our own beliefs, desires, and passions. Why should our projections onto everyday life be any different?

At many moments of watching a movie we are both completely caught up in the characters and events portrayed *and* also aware that it is just a movie, literally a simultaneous projection in two realities or states of awareness. Watching movies seems actually to develop our ability to inhabit two realities at the same time in a way that was probably much less developed in post-tribal secular modern individuals before popular film spread around the world. So watching movies may not be so very different from what the traditions like Buddhism that stress mindfulness call *being aware of being aware*, and it is an ability these traditions have always purposefully sought to develop in human consciousness. Why? Because it is precisely that awareness of awareness that is needed in order both to be fully involved in the present *and* to retain the background awareness of space, without which we live in a flat material plane, cut off from the possibility of transcendence to any higher order of perception.

It is true as well that as everyday life becomes increasingly indistinguishable from an action/horror flick playing 24/7—living in a state of world crisis, economic near-collapse, and the falling away of long-held securities and certainties—a desire or need arises in many of us for knowledge about other dimensions of being, particularly those we suspect might lie beyond this "real" one. In such times, the great movies, and particularly the classic transit movies, can provide a grounding unity; they remind our fractured society of the truths we all know and the goodness we all yearn for. We give our love to these movies because they mirror back the lives we all recognize and participate in and often teach us ways to transcend our lack of progression, our limitations. Showing both sides, these movies provide everyday examples of our inability or failure to transcend physical reality and of our ability to recognize that everything is a dream, a play of light and shadow. They show that we as humans each have a personal destiny and a task or some action we need to complete in order to fulfill it. So the great movies bring us together. They entrance us; for a time we forget ourselves and identify completely with the characters and their story, and yet we can be aware, at least in the deep background, that it is all a movie, insubstantial as a dream but nevertheless functioning as a tool for our enlightenment, showing us the entire human pageant—all the different roles and situations that can exist, the endless scenarios played out in dealing with the problem of suffering and death.

In *The Republic*, Plato uses the metaphor of a cave to sum up his view of an ignorant humanity, trapped in the depths of delusion, unaware even of its own limited perspective. Through the beneficence of grace, accumulated merit for positive actions, or the intervention of heavenly powers, rare individuals escape the limited confines of that cave and in the arduous struggle to fulfill the dictum inscribed in the Temple of Apollo at Delphi, "Know Thyself," arrive at a higher perception of reality in its essential form—the unity of the One—the Good, the True, and the Beautiful.[1]

> If he were living today, Plato might replace his rather awkward cave metaphor with a movie theater, with the projector replacing the fire, the film replacing the objects which cast shadows, the shadows on the cave wall with the projected movie on the screen, and the echo with the loudspeakers behind the screen. The essential point is that the prisoners in the cave are not seeing reality, but only a shadowy representation of it. The importance of the allegory lies in Plato's belief that there are invisible truths lying under the apparent surface of things which only the most enlightened can grasp. Used to the world of illusion in the cave, the prisoners at first resist enlightenment, as students resist education. . . . At the end of the passage, Plato expresses another of his favorite ideas: that education is not a process of putting knowledge into empty minds, but of making people realize that which they already know.[2]

In a way, movies provoke this function of recollection, reminding us of the Good, the True, and the Beautiful by which we wish to live our lives. Movies, like classic Greek tragedies, often serve as tools to excavate the deep and sometimes dark contents of our own minds, familiarizing us with that content so that consciousness is no longer seduced and alarmed by it but can appreciate and profit in accepting those images as part of its learning process.[3] Further, by projecting the multitudinous possibilities of a thousand characters and lifetimes before us, movies can serve in the functional parameters of the expansion of consciousness. The mind's identification and nonidentification with the cinematic illusion can acquaint consciousness with a seemingly endless array of internal snares and shams, the mind-field of its deepest beliefs, judgments, and appropriations, leading us to a deeper understanding of what we believe about, and how we relate to, our suffering, ultimately freeing that consciousness on its journey toward its rightful destiny. Movies, then, can function the same way as other approaches to the dynamics of the human mind described by the Dalai Lama—as "a precious gateway into the alleviation of suffering, which I believe to be our principal task on this earth."[4]

Powerfully able to convey the deepest emotions shared by all individuals—our dreams, desires, and concerns about the fundamental meaning of life, love, birth, and death—movies are able to produce a shared resonance among all humans. And beyond any doubt, the deepest and most mysterious of human concerns is, and always has been, about death and what lies beyond.

Chapter Fifteen

THE BARDO OF EXISTENCE

Birth

Modern civilization . . . is largely devoted to the pursuit of the cult of delusion. There is no general information about the nature of mind. It is hardly ever written about by writers or intellectuals; modern philosophers do not speak of it directly; the majority of scientists deny it could possibly be there at all. It plays no part in popular culture: No one sings about it, no one talks about it in plays, and it's not on TV. We are actually educated into believing that nothing is real beyond what we can perceive with our ordinary senses.

—Sogyal Rinpoche

Sean's voice over dark screen: "OK, let me say this . . . If I lost my wife and, uh, the next day a little bird landed on my windowsill, looked me right in the eye, and in plain English said, 'Sean, it's me, Anna, I'm back,' what could I say? I guess I'd believe her. Or I'd want to. I'd be stuck with a bird (audience laughter). But, other than that, no, I'm a man of science. I just don't believe that mumbo jumbo. Now that's gonna have to be the last question. I need to go running before I head home."

A snow-coated trail in Central Park: A slightly elevated tracking shot trails the jogging, hooded Sean from behind; Alexandre Desplat's haunting score rhythmically pulsates with the steady gait of the runner.

Main title appears over the scene—BIRTH: Sean approaches and enters a darkened tunnel but does not come out; the camera slowly dollies in toward his prostrate body—dead—a heart attack.

Cut: A newborn infant is lifted out of water.

Ten years later: Guests arrive at the fashionable East Side apartment of Eleanor (Lauren Bacall), a sharp-witted and commanding matriarch, mother of Sean's widow, Anna (Nicole Kidman). The event is Anna's engagement to Joseph (Danny Huston), who has been courting her for a number of years. We see Clifford (Peter Stormare), who was Sean's best friend, and his wife, Clara (Anne Heche), arriving in the lobby. There is also a stranger, a young boy about ten (Cameron Bright), sitting on a bench by the elevator. Clara, saying she needs to get her gift for Anna wrapped, sends Clifford on to the party. She leaves and walks into a park, unaware she is being followed by the young boy. There, she buries the supposed gift beneath some leaves and returns to the engagement party.

Some days later, Eleanor's apartment: An intimate gathering celebrating Eleanor's birthday is attended by her immediate family: Anna and her fiancé, Joseph; Anna's pregnant sister, Laura (Alison Elliott), and her husband, Bob (Arliss Howard); and a close family friend, Mrs. Hill (Zoe Caldwell). A stranger, the same boy who had followed Clara into the park at the engagement party, arrives with a message for the future bride. When the boy, also named Sean, like Anna's dead husband, insists on seeing Anna, the guests are mostly amused. "Someone's playing a joke!" they comment. Lee (Novella Nelson), the family maid, is immediately alert to some impending danger, but Anna is curious enough to take young Sean into the privacy of another room, where he delivers his message: "It's me, your husband. I'm Sean." Uncertain how to respond, Anna reacts to the boy with a combination of curiosity, amusement, and caution. As Sean persists in his story she becomes mildly irritated, eventually marching him to the doorman in the lobby and asking him to send the boy home in a cab. Her irritation becomes a curious foreboding with Sean's parting words, "You'll be making a big mistake if you marry Joseph." Anna is not quite able to shake off her disquiet but manages to share a sisterly giggle when she reveals the boy's message to Laura. In the following scene Anna and Joseph make love in their bedroom at Eleanor's apartment.

The next morning Anna receives a note in the apartment lobby but doesn't open it until she returns home. It simply says, "Don't marry Joseph. Sean." Even though they are going to the opera, Joseph is sufficiently soured by the note to insist on seeing the boy's father, in front of whom he repeatedly attempts to extract a promise from Sean: "Tell her that you will never see her or bother her again." Sean repeatedly insists, "I can't." Even as it is becoming increasing clear to Anna that Sean is unable to say the words, the boy collapses. As Joseph and Anna leave for the opera, Joseph quietly says to her, "Well done." But the look on Anna's face reflects the ferment within. A full two-minute close-up of Anna's face while the opera orchestra plays the ominous "Prologue" to act 1 of *Die Walküre* reveals the tangle of fragmented thoughts and conflicted feelings raging through her psyche.

The following day Anna lunches with her mother. Eleanor lets it be known that Sean called and left Anna a message: "Meet me in the park. You know where!" In the park she finds Sean at the very spot of her husband's death. In this moment the tension of her conflict relaxes, and she opens to the possibility that the boy is indeed Sean reborn. The truth about whether the boy is or is not her reincarnated husband recedes behind her more immediate experience of an unfamiliar energetic dimension cracking through layers of uncertainty and self-doubt, as well as the conventional strictures of her sheltered world—a world devoted to the pursuit of illusion because she has been educated into believing that nothing is real beyond what can be perceived with her ordinary senses. Breaking through those strictures, she enters a bizarre, quasi-miraculous state that renders her vulnerable to the seduction of a return to her own past life. In that life, whatever was wrong about her marriage, whatever she cannot let go of, will be made right. In transit terms, Anna is making a last, desperate attempt to run from rather than recognize her internal contradictions—the surest road to hell.

Actually, in many ways Anna is more of a child than Sean. She has never separated from her mother and her mother's home. She is always led by others. Joseph would be the perfect husband—a paternal figure who tells her what to do and what to think. Having spent ten years as a young widow, she has yet to work through her relationship with the dead Sean. Joseph is practically dragging her toward a new marriage, and she appears to have no real life of her own. Lacking the maturity to deal with either real life or real death, she is literally stuck in between, the very definition of transit. As we've seen, actual death is not the only trigger for the transit state. In psychological terms Anna is dying to her identity as Sean's wife and seeking rebirth as Joseph's wife. The options she perceives in her transit experience seem to be either to accept Sean's death and get on with life or to find a way to return to her relationship with Sean in the person of the boy and recreate that as an opportunity for fulfillment. So the childlike Anna meets the child Sean, who is in many ways more mature than she. Unlike Anna, who is pushed and pulled by everyone else's ideas and opinions, Sean has a strong sense of himself. While he is thoroughly grounded in a conviction of who he is (Anna's husband) and what he wants (Anna), that conviction is unfortunately mitigated by the peculiar limitations of his own transit experience, specifically the fragmentary knowledge of his own memory. Still, he is undeterred by anyone's attempts to silence or dismiss him. So there are two odd pairings: the physical woman Anna with the child Sean and the emotional child Anna with the more resolute Sean, neither configuration providing much possibility of a favorable outcome.

Nevertheless, Anna feels driven to make her relationship with Sean work. Her first project is to convince the family; she has her brother-in-law, Bob, a doctor (society's high priest), question the boy to prove he really is her husband. Of course young Sean answers all the personal questions about his marriage to Anna and provides little-known details about Anna's life with an uncanny accuracy, down to the most private of secrets, such as who told Anna there wasn't a Santa Claus. This turn of events drives Joseph and the family into deeper levels of confusion and conflict while simultaneously reinforcing Anna's belief in Sean.

Desperate, Anna visits Clifford and Clara, whom we met at Joseph and Anna's engagement party when Clara mysteriously left to bury a package, said to be a gift for Anna, in the park. Anna begins with, "I met somebody who seems to be Sean." A jumble of raw emotions and fragmented thoughts pours out, ramblings on being unable to get the dead Sean out of her system, rationalizations of her love for Joseph, a mishmash of matrimonial and maternal emotions, and then an attempt to express what overwhelmed her about the boy when he collapsed: "And then it hit me. I'm falling in love with Sean again. That's what's happening." Clifford and Clara's reaction to this display is somewhere between "Give me a break" and cautious concern. Clifford knew the dead Sean better than anyone, knew him for what he really had been—Clfford was best man at Sean and Anna's wedding. Clara is suspicious for a darker reason: she was Sean's lover, simultaneously betraying both Anna and Clifford. Anna asks for Clifford's help—she needs him to tell the boy to go away because she can't do it herself. We see that the level of confusion at work in Anna's mind is growing despite *and* because of her unspoken hope that the boy is indeed her husband.

Anna meets Sean at school: New York on a sunny spring afternoon. Like playacting children, they speak intimately over ice cream about sex. She wonders how they can possibly live together, how he can support her, and asks, "How will you satisfy my needs?"

Sean: I know what you are talking about.

Anna: Have you ever been with a girl?

Sean (gallantly): You'd be the first.

Then, in some comic/grotesque mimicry of a classic Hollywood love story, they ride a carriage though Central Park. Anna must return home for the wedding rehearsal, and she brings the boy with her. As she soaks in a hot bath, the boy enters, undresses, and gets into the tub with her. There is a cut to Joseph entering the bedroom. His hand goes for the bathroom door. He hesitates and walks away.[1]

Once again to the strains of Wagner, played now pizzicato by a string quartet, the wedding-rehearsal participants sit listening to *Here Comes the Bride*. Joseph sits in the first row. Sean has somehow been placed directly behind him and, keeping time with the music, is absentmindedly foot-tapping the back of Joseph's chair. An irritated Joseph turns around and tells him to stop. But as the beat of the music continues, Sean keeps pace with his rhythmic kicking of the chair. Joseph explodes. All the frustration and anger that has been building since Sean's appearance, reinforced now by his experience of Sean as a sexual rival, manifests in an explosive rage and a need to punish the boy. It takes half the wedding party to restrain him. The room in a shambles, Joseph is led away by friends. His unraveling seems to release Anna's remaining inhibitions regarding Sean, who has fled the apartment into the street. Anna follows him, and we witness the two in an erotic embrace and kiss. They return to the apartment, and when Clifford arrives, late for the rehearsal, Sean runs to him and hugs him as if for protection from Joseph. Clifford seems, as usual, befuddled, as if he might completely disintegrate with just an iota more of ambiguity in his life. He arbitrarily tells Anna that the boy is not Sean; she insists that he is. Clara arrives and Sean lets her into the house. She has dirty hands (implying she has just come from attempting to retrieve the package we saw her bury in the park) and orders Sean to take her to the bathroom. Like some dominatrix, she orders him to come in and, after washing her hands, tells him to dry them. We get the flavor of what her relationship with the dead Sean may have been like. She tells the boy she has a new address and writes it on his hand. Sean nervously says, "Don't tell Anna."

There is a brief scene in Eleanor's kitchen. Both Eleanor and Laura are telling Anna she must send Sean home, implying that what she is doing is child molestation. Anna goes to her bedroom, where Sean is sleeping, and tucks him in, accentuating her growing confusion between maternal and sexual feelings. Next we see Sean and Anna in the back seat of a taxi, returning the boy to his home. Sean's head rests on Anna's lap. She is stroking his hair affectionately and reassuring him that she is going to tell his mother everything is okay. Sean asks, "Then what?" She responds that she doesn't know, "But I'm thinking." There is a close-up on the boy's face and a slow dissolve into a flashback of that curious scene early in the movie at the engagement party where Clara makes the excuse to leave the apartment lobby because she needs to get Anna's gift wrapped. We see, once again, Clara heading into the park, secretly followed by the boy Sean. She steps off the pathway into a leafy area and buries what seems to be Anna's gift beneath some loose dirt and dead leaves.

Cut: Clara pacing back and forth in her apartment. Sean sits at a kitchen table.

Cut: Back to the earlier park scene; the boy is holding a packet of letters and is reading one.

Cut: Back to Clara pacing, the boy at the table.

Clara (petulantly):   You're not Sean!

Sean: Yes I am.

Clara: When you opened the door for me yesterday I knew you weren't Sean.

Sean: Who are you?

Clara: I'm your lover.

Sean: Anna's my lover.

Clara: I'm your lover. Anna's your wife! If you had been Sean, and I had hoped you were, you would have come to me first. (*Pause, staring intensely at Sean*) And I would have explored this. But you didn't. Are they in your bag?

What *is* in Sean's ragged little backpack are indeed Anna's letters to her husband, who had given them, unopened, to Clara in order, as Clara vaingloriously proclaims, "to prove that he loved me more." Clara had intended to give the letters as a gift of hate to Anna at her betrothal, but she couldn't do it. Clara is certainly narcissistic—cold, calculating, complex—but not stupid. It is unlikely she would succumb to pride, envy, or even hatred enough to do something as lacking in benefit to herself as giving Anna the unread love letters simply out of malice. In fact, she reveals just how human she is by reclaiming the letters that we now know had been retrieved and read by the boy. So Clara sits gloating with her trophies, denying the boy's claim to being her ex-lover. Her final words to him are, "Sorry kid, you're not him." A devastated Sean flees her apartment, returns to the park and, as young boys are wont to do, climbs a tree. Fade to black.

When Anna returns to her apartment she finds a very dirty boy in her tub, apparently from climbing a tree in Central Park and then running away from policemen trying to find out where he lives. She doesn't know about his visit to Clara and is even more swept up in the drama of the reincarnated Sean and the immediate problem of how to resume their marital relationship. Her over-the-edge plan is to for them to go someplace where they are unknown, live together until he is twenty-one, then marry and pick life up where it left off when he died. Even more than surrendering, she now welcomes as blessed fate this special destiny with Sean.

Anna has surrendered to the illusion of the transit world! She is unable to free herself from her idealized memory of life with her dead husband, unable to acknowledge that relationship's failure to support her separation from a dominant mother or her growth into an autonomous person, and, above all, unable to acknowledge Sean's essential betrayal of their marriage. Her ten years of widowhood reveal more about her failure and anxiety as a woman than her grief for Sean. Her grief is for herself. The boy promises Anna salvation, an apparent gift from the beyond offering her the seduction of returning to her past life, only in a different form. She invests the boy with the positive energy of an idealized husband so that she doesn't have to die into the full awareness of impermanence and loss. So Anna continues to lay out her plan to the dirty boy in her tub. She stares at him adoringly and declares, "I love you, Sean."

"I'm not Sean," he replies, his head and body sinking beneath the water. And in truth, since his deliverance by Clara, he is not *that* Sean anymore.

Anna stares in disbelief at his submerged body and pulls him up from the water.

Sean: I'm not Sean because I love you.

Anna: You make no sense.

Sean: I can't explain it to you better.

138

Anna: You're going to have to.

Sean: Can I please have a towel, Anna? I have to put my clothes back
on. My mother is going to be here soon.

For Sean, the spell is over. For Anna, it is shattered.

We were not alone in wondering why this film is called *Birth*. It
certainly begins with the husband Sean speculating on the possibility
of reincarnation. We then see him collapse on a running path and die,
immediately followed by the scene of a newborn child being lifted out
of water. So, while it seems that the intended theme of the film is that
of rebirth, we never again see a birth, except of course what might be
called Sean's symbolic second rebirth when Anna pulls him up from
his submersion in the bathtub—his rebirth into being his fated self,
no longer believing himself Anna's Sean. From our perspective—how
the various forms and functions of transit/bardo manifest in a popular
art form—*Birth* is about the process of the boy Sean's birth, or, more
accurately, his births.

There is an old tale that we come into each incarnation ignorant
of our past lives because, just before we are born, an angel lays a finger
over our lips and we lose all memory of what went before. This angelic
touch, the story goes, is why we all have an indentation above our lips.
In the case of young Sean, the angel's touch didn't quite take.[2] By fate or
circumstance ordained, he, at the age of ten, is awakened to his identity
as Anna's husband in a previous life, seemingly triggered by Clara and
her letters. And though in that life he had been involved in an adulterous
affair and treated Anna very shabbily, the boy remembers clearly only
what he has assimilated from those letters: her highly idealized longing
and love for him. He thinks only of how to be joined to that sense of
perfect union promised by the desperate needs and desires expressed in
her letters.

We have seen any number of reviews that rationalized the plot with possession and exorcism and/or raised the specter of psychoanalysis. We were not moved. More helpful, we found, in trying to put together the pieces of a film its director referred to as a "mystery of the heart,"[3] was to delve deeper into the workings of the bardos, concentrating on three of them, beginning with the bardo of dying, which contains the period from the beginning of the dissolution of the physical elements of mind and body to actual death, with its terror of annihilation, then on to the bardo of dharmata, a confrontation, for better or worse, with one's own essential nature as manifested by peaceful and wrathful deities; assaulted from every direction by demonic visions of one's negative karma—unresolved residues of lust, anger, pride, deceit, envy, and fear—one is made increasingly aware of fear and hopelessness. Then, finally, in the bardo of existence either liberation or, if one is not liberated, the process of entry into a womb and rebirth is determined. We suggest that the period between Sean's death in the tunnel and the scene of Anna pulling the young Sean up from the water of his bath is the time/space continuum within which the two Seans exist as one in these three bardos—that is the essence of *Birth*.

Returning to the film, the word *May* appears on the screen imposed over the formal garden of a country home, and we are reminded that Joseph and Anna's wedding was to be in May at Eleanor's beach house. Assembled guests stroll about. The wedding photographer is having a difficult time getting Anna to pose for a single shot. She seems distressed, even distraught. Joseph watches her from a distance with growing concern. We cut to a scene of another place, another photographer taking pictures, but of individual children at a grade school, perhaps for a yearbook. Over this scene a boy's voice narrates what seems to be a letter: "Dear Anna, Thanks for your letter . . . I'm really happy being back in school and my friends don't know what happened. So it's okay

... I'm seeing an expert. They said I'd been imagining things. Mom said maybe it was a spell ... "

On the screen Sean sits for his photograph and smiles for the first time in the film. "Tell everyone that I'm sorry that I caused trouble for them ... They said the good thing is that nothing happened. Well, guess I'll see you in another lifetime. Sean."

Cut back to the wedding. At some point Anna has wandered away from the guests, and we see her, still in her wedding gown, standing in the ocean, her face distorted with anguish. Joseph leads her away from the waves and her desperate attempt to reenter the water, die, and seek her own rebirth. However reluctantly, she consents to Joseph and leans on him as they walk off down the beach, together, alone. Anna, for the present, is led away from death and toward—what? Her dependency unresolved, more of a helpless, demoralized child than ever, she is trapped in transit, pretty much where she began—confused, out of control, and ambivalent toward life, wandering in the bardo of this life.

You might think this shot would be a good place for the film to end. And indeed, with the distant image of Joseph and Anna diminishing in the ocean mist, the film fades to black. The music fades as well, and with just the sound of crashing waves the main credits come up—stars, producers, writers, director, and then the main title, *Birth*, as even the waves dissolve into silence. But director Jonathan Glazer has not quite finished playing with our minds. A few beats of silence, and we are hit with the dopey pop song *Tonight You Belong To Me*, written in the 1930s but making the charts in a 1956 recording sung by Patience and Prudence. Recall the drawn-out first lines of the song:

> I know owowowowowowow
> you belongggggg
> to somebody new
> But tonight you belongggg to me.

141

The irony is delicious. That the song's artists are named Patience and Prudence (Joseph and Anna) doubles our pleasure, doubles our fun. It also serves as Glazer's tribute to Stanley Kubrick, reflecting that director's darkest seriocomic films, *Lolita* and *Dr. Strangelove*. One sly wag commented that *Birth* is "the best Stanley Kubrick film not made by Kubrick."[4] But even more essentially, it connects us to the spirit of the transit world, a world beyond comedy and tragedy, good and bad, a world that basically exists as the projections of one's own mind—whatever exists in your real life, or even in the reel life of movies, will be projected into the *experience* of transit.

Birth is controversial on any number of levels. Critics had a field day with it, loving or hating it, with few in between. The notion of reincarnation is challenging for many.[5] Recall Sean's offscreen words to his audience at the very beginning of the film: "I'm a man of science. I just don't believe that mumbo jumbo." Glazer has been quoted as saying, "We aimed to make something robust in which every question leads to another. I'm not a Buddhist and I don't believe in reincarnation; I don't think I could do a film about it if I did. I was more interested in the idea of eternal love. I wanted to make a mystery, the mystery of the heart."[6] But denials aside, as evidenced by both his first film, *Sexy Beast* (2001), and *Birth* (2004), his second, we suspect that Glazer is nothing if not a master trickster. Many critics attempted to force some alternative diagnosis on the events witnessed on the screen, often creating their own type of convoluted but more conventional logic. Many of the blog comments on *Birth* were penned from a psychological perspective; the film lends itself readily to such analysis (which might be good for Anna, but for young Sean we prescribe a giggling Tibetan Buddhist monk). The problem with most psychological interpretations of *Birth* is that they betray the very spirit of the film—the sheer gleeful malice of Glazer's ability to push what is possible beyond not what we imagine, but what we *can* imagine. To do that is to create magnificent cinema.

Nonetheless, we believe that *Birth* is best observed, as is the custom for all drama, with a willing suspension of disbelief. That accomplished, the film rewards us in its capacity to suggest new ways to experience different levels of reality, more transcendent levels of reality, possibly even transit realities, where anything and everything is possible. Maybe psychological analysis completely misses the point. Who knows how these things work? Why *can't* the movie be totally about some sort of makeshift reincarnation? After all, wasn't it Sigmund Freud, the great granddaddy of all psychology, who said, "Sometimes a cigar is just a cigar"?

Chapter Sixteen

SENTIMENTAL JOURNEY ON A SPIRITUAL PATH

Hereafter

Modern America, Christian or not, has ineluctably retreated to the position of the pagan philosophers of late antiquity: Our souls are Immortal by nature; all will be saved, it just may take some souls longer to figure out that altruism and moral behavior are what guarantees salvation—or alternatively, that it is really self-realization that guarantees our salvation. Either seems acceptable as a statement of the distinctively American hereafter because each validates quintessentially American values in this life.

—Alan F. Segal

If you are anything like us, you were probably excited about what director Clint Eastwood's foray into the beyond, *Hereafter* (2010), was going to add to what other films had already told us about that inevitable transition from life to something beyond. After all, Eastwood has been described as being one of Hollywood's sharpest "bullshit detectors," so for us it was a must-see, but for more than just our abiding interest in the subject of transit. It promised us a fresh look at the genre we both love by a master of his craft: the perfect way to further our story of how

Hollywood has presented its musings on the seemingly unknowable phenomenon of navigating your way to an existence beyond death, popularly called the hereafter.

The Warner Brothers Pictures logo, followed by the now-famous Malpaso Productions logo, appears on the screen backed by the romantic strains of a very mellow jazz guitar. Eastwood is credited as the film's music composer, but we are immediately aware this score wasn't composed by Dirty Harry. We are hearing the other Eastwood, the sentimental one who moved us with the very cool song selection and score of *The Bridges of Madison County*. On the screen appears a gorgeous tropical seascape, projecting a mood of romance, but romance as the subtext of some larger domain of sentiments—things held dear to the heart. The title, *Hereafter*, superimposed over the scene presents us with the idea of the spiritual domain—things based on our beliefs and hopes. As we shall see, these two domains, sentimental and spiritual, are often confused. We see Marie (Cécile de France), a popular television journalist, together with her lover and producer, Didier (Thierry Neuvic), waking in a beautiful hotel overlooking a calm early morning sea. Marie is off for some early shopping, leaving Didier in bed. As she browses pleasantly through some quaint street shops, her attention is drawn by distant loud cries and confused activity; a tsunami has hit the island and is bearing down on her and those rushing past in their haste to escape the crushing wall of water and debris only seconds away. There is no escape. Marie struggles to stay above the rushing flood but is struck on the head and pulled under. We see her unconscious body floating eerily amid the debris. Pulled from the water, seemingly lifeless, she is left for dead, and we see her experiencing herself walking amid shadowed figures toward a brilliant white light. We have seen this light in many of the films discussed so far and realize that Marie is having a near-death experience (NDE).[1] But she is revived and gasps back to life.

Dazed, but alive, she wanders through the rubble of the disaster and eventually connects with Didier.

Back in Paris Marie finds that her preoccupation with her NDE is diminishing her capacity to be an effective television commentator. Didier suggests that she take some time off to follow up on an offer to write a book on ex-president Mitterrand. She pursues that option, but soon realizes that her experience of the beyond has become the dominant reality of her life and that what she really needs and wants is to explore the possibility of life on the other side, the hereafter. A daunting task, but as Alan F. Segal points out, "The afterlife is another way to express the same transcendent, non-confirmable issue of God. . . . The very speculation that an afterlife exists seems like a human need and an ideal—again like love, beauty or justice—that exist in our minds rather than the world and gives a sense of meaning to our lives. Like beauty and justice, life after death is no less important for being unverifiable."[2]

In San Francisco, George Lonegan (Matt Damon) reluctantly gives in to his brother Billy's pressure on him to do a psychic reading for a wealthy potential client, Christos. George has a gift—which is also his curse—a genuine ability to communicate with the dead. He has tried to earn his living as a medium, but the emotional residue of his sessions eventually left him a wreck. The well-meaning Billy sees George's gift as an asset that can make both of them very wealthy. George is a good man, but his psyche is shattered; his boundaries have crumbled, and it is difficult for him to say no to Billy. Christos is amazed by George's reading, but George is devastated. Indeed, to live in modern secular times, in a dynamic future-obsessed environment, must be enormously challenging if your calling happens, like George's, to be that of a shaman. Traditionally (and we are talking since Paleolithic times, predating all organized religion) shamanism has encompassed the belief that shamans are intermediaries or messengers between the living world and the spiritual worlds, between life and death. One doesn't decide to become a shaman: the task calls you. The calling usually begins with an initiatory crisis, a rite of passage involving physical illness or psychological crisis. George had both: an illness that pushed him to the brink of death and insanity. For a while he was diagnosed as schizophrenic. Traditionally, shamans gain knowledge and the power to heal by entering the spiritual world. For George, the connection to that world is by touch. By holding his client's hand he can communicate with the spirit of the deceased in question. These sessions leave him both emotionally and physically drained, and the rest of his life, with few friends and no love interest, doesn't seem to provide him with real sustenance. When things become too stressful he retreats into listening to audio books, specifically Derek Jacobi's recordings of the Dickens novels—a vicarious life in another time and realm.

In London, twelve-year-old twins Marcus and Jason (Frankie and George McLaren) scramble to avoid Child Protection Services, which wants to remove them from their home and their heroin-addicted mother, Jackie (Lyndsey Marshal). There is, in spite of the dysfunctionality, a deep love and connection between them and their mother. After they evade the latest crisis, Jason goes to pick up detox drugs for his mother and is killed by a van while trying to avoid street thugs. Marcus is devastated by having his brother torn from him; moreover, his mother is committed for treatment, and he is sent to a foster home.

Back in San Francisco, George enrolls in an Italian cooking class and gets paired with a somewhat superficial but chipper young woman named Melanie. She is on the rebound after an abandoned-at-the-altar experience in Pittsburgh. They are attracted to each other and after the following week's class decide to cook an Italian dinner at George's place. Things are going well until George fails to intercept a call from his brother in time to block a message revealing that he is a psychic reader. Melanie's curiosity is aroused, and she prompts him to reveal some of the more personal aspects of his life, including his childhood illness, bout with schizophrenia, near-death experiences, and subsequent acquisition of psychic skills. He talks about his visions and the fact that he has medication to stop them but doesn't take it because it leaves him unable to feel anything. Melanie presses him for a reading, which should set off "Don't Go There" alarms. But George, though not stupid, is desperate and so starved for connection that he forges into Melanie's swamp and is soon in well over his head. Holding her hand, he contacts the spirits of Melanie's mother and her father, who ends the session by asking her forgiveness for what he did to her as a child. Her fragile composure completely shattered, Melanie flees the house. A rueful George considers a tranquilizer but chooses to retreat into Dickens's world with his audio books

In England the officiating minister at Jason's funeral delivers a string of platitudes about how Jason is in heaven looking down upon us, et cetera, et cetera, while ignoring the hellish realm of suffering for those in mourning, most particularly Marcus. The minister hastily delivers an urn of ashes to Marcus and hurries off to the next in an impersonal assembly line of funerals. Marcus has an affecting meeting with his mother, currently deemed not competent to care for him, in which she acknowledges her need to sort herself out and promises not to abandon him. We sense her genuine desire to be a good-enough mother. Marcus is fortunate, as well, in having a pair of caring social workers and a safe and sane foster home with people who really care. They even arrange for him to have a second bed in his room, on which, when he isn't wearing it, he places his greatest treasure, Jason's cap. His basic needs covered, Marcus begins to explore the Internet. He googles "Death" and finds an entry for Islam, "The Angel of Death will find you"; another for Christianity, "If you believe in Christ you will have nothing to fear"; and yet more. He shakes his head; this information isn't telling him what he needs to know. He also steals money from his foster parents in order to find a psychic in London who will help him contact Jason. What he finds is a string of fakes, phonies, frauds, and, even sadder, well-meaning but deluded do-gooders. While waiting for a train in London's underground Charring Cross Station, Marcus is jostled by the crowd, causing him to lose Jason's cap, the sacred talisman he wears constantly. He retrieves the cap but misses his train. Within seconds of the train's departure there is an explosion in the darkened tunnel. Because of the cap, Marcus escapes almost certain death.

In her search for the meaning of her near-death experience Marie has parted ways with Didier, whose reply when asked what he thinks happens when you die is, "The lights go out, that's it"—direct and brutal. He has also replaced Marie in his bed. Marie's research on the NDE takes her to a hospice high in the Swiss Alps and to its director (Marthe Keller), a former atheist whose long experience of working with the dying has convinced her that the afterlife is genuine. She encourages Marie to pursue her research and to write a book that will convince the scientific community to accept the afterlife as a reality.

Back in San Francisco, laid off from his factory job and unable to deal with the pressure of his brother Billy's blandishments to involve him in setting up a psychic-consulting business, George boards a plane for England. There, visiting the Dickens House, he spies a poster announcing a live reading by Derek Jacobi of Dickens's *Little Dorrit* at the London Book Fair that very day. As fate would have it, Marcus and his foster parents are also at the fair. There too is Marie, promoting her now-published book, *Hereafter: A Conspiracy of Silence*. George, attracted to her table, purchases a copy and while receiving the book touches her hand, causing him to experience an immediate flash of Marie's near-death experience. Almost simultaneously, Marcus, who remembers George's face from his Internet search for psychics, spots him and attempts to talk with him about Jason. George, still discombobulated by his flash of Marie's near-death experience, brushes him off and heads for his hotel.

Marcus follows him but is unable to get into the hotel, so he stands patiently on the street below George's window. George eventually gives in, brings the boy to his room and, taking his hands, does a reading. It is a powerful moment in the film. Through George, Marcus experiences Jason as he was—confident, protective, and loving. Jason wants Marcus to live his own life, not a shadow life of himself. That's why he knocked the hat off in the tube station. Saving Marcus from the bombing was a welcome side effect. Marcus interrupts, "I don't want to be here without you." George gives voice to Jason: "If you're worried about being on your own, don't be, because you're not. Because he is you and you are him. One cell! One person! Always!" With this declaration of the essential unity of all things, George realizes there is nothing more to say.

Later, Marcus has a reunion with his mother, who seems well on her way to recovery. He is not wearing Jason's cap. That evening George answers the phone and hears the voice of Marcus: "Mayfair." To George's "What?" he responds, "The hotel where she is staying." There is a pause. "The woman you like." George calls Marie's hotel and leaves a message for her. We don't hear the message, but she looks pleased when she hears it.

Cut to the next day. Marie is looking for George at an outdoor café. He sees her first, and as he does he has a vision of kissing her. He stands and calls out her name. They shake hands and George is aware that there is no flash, no vision. Perhaps the curse that came with his gift is gone. They walk away together.

Hereafter was not a critical success. The consensus was, "Despite a thought-provoking premise and Clint Eastwood's typical flair as director, *Hereafter* fails to generate much compelling drama, straddling the line between poignant sentimentality and hokey tedium."[3]

But then, much of what passes for criticism can be facile and simplistic, sometimes blatantly so. Nevertheless we partially agree; what is straddled is the line between sentimentality and spirituality mentioned earlier—the often-blurred line between sentiments, things held dear to the heart, and spirituality, things based on our faith and hope. While various characteristics of both can often appear analogous, it helps to remember that the sentimental achieves fulfillment horizontally while the spiritual achieves fulfillment vertically. Having seen Marcus receive Jason's gift from the beyond, the essential truth of the unity of all things—All is one!—we sense that the depth of that message will guide him to his highest possible realization. We wonder how Marie and George will fare. She has her vision and her book, her compilation of what she thinks others should think. Can she nurture that into true wisdom? George has his own wealth of spiritual experience. Does that make for a fortunate incarnation? Can he learn to contain the downsides, move out of the hell world he has inhabited to the next level, that of purgatory, where he can experience the suffering that leads to no suffering? Together, can they generate from their experiences a true sense of existing as spiritual beings?

Borrowing some words used earlier in this book, earthly love is love of a subject for its object. It reflects the inherent separation perceived by the thinking mind and the senses. Heavenly love is the love of Being for itself, that which is one with everything—no duality of subject and object. In the fires of purgatory, earthly love transmutes to heavenly love. We wish Marie and George well and leave them with these down-to-earth, practical words from Carol Zaleski's *Otherworld Journeys*: "Whatever the study of near-death visions might reveal about the experience of death, it teaches us just as much about ourselves as image-making and image-bound beings. To admit this is no concession to the debunkers; on the contrary, by recognizing the imaginative character of otherworld visions, we move beyond the merely defensive posture of arguing against reductionism. Within the limits here discussed we are able to grant the validity of near-death experiences as one way in which the religious imagination mediates the search for ultimate truth."[4]

Chapter Seventeen

OUR NEXT-TO-ALL-TIME FAVORITE

Casablanca

> *It's still the same old story*
> *A fight for love and glory*
> *A tale of do or die. . . .*
> *The fundamental things apply*
> *As time goes by.*
>
> —Herman Hupfeld

Casablanca (1942), one of the most enduringly popular movies ever made in Hollywood, is beloved by generation after generation for its romanticism, stirring patriotism, spirit of transcendence, and unforgettable lines, even the often-misquoted "Play it, Sam." Like so many transit films, it contains more than the sum of its talented writers, actors, and technicians. It has a life and a power that achieves its own state of transcendence through its recognition of a deeply held inner truth—the truth of freedom—and exquisitely transmits the spirit of that freedom. A large number of the cast and crew, including those playing Nazis, were in fact German Jews who had escaped from Hitler's Germany. Conrad Veidt, ironically the movie's villain, had narrowly escaped an SS death squad sent after him for his anti-Nazi activities. Other notable refugees in the film are Peter Lorre and S. K. Sakall. The supporting cast also brought to a dozen small roles an understanding and a desperation that could never have come from central casting—it is said that during filming of the famous scene in Rick's café when "La Marseillaise" is sung over the German song "Die Wacht Am Rhein," many of the actors had real tears in their eyes, overcome by the emotions the scene brought out. Given the times and those involved, *Casablanca* was a keenly focused expression of the deepest feelings of literally millions of displaced and war-ravaged individuals.[1]

For us, *Casablanca*'s place in the pantheon of transit films is unmistakable. Consider: Right from the beginning we are told about the tortuous trail of resisters and refugees from Paris to Marseilles to Oran and across the rim of Africa to French Morocco and Casablanca, from where they hope they can eventually move on to a new life, perhaps even in America, the land of the free. But, meanwhile, in Casablanca they "wait and wait and wait." Casablanca is in a sense removed from the war in Europe, yet it is influenced by the presence of occupying Nazis and their Vichy minions. It has become a place of transit, between lives left behind and lives hoped for in the future, lived somewhere else, somewhere better. Almost none of the refugees want to stay in Casablanca. What they want is to get out and move on safely to their new lives.

Like the transit realm itself, Casablanca seems arbitrary, dangerous, and confusing. We see the local police arresting a man about whom we know nothing except that "his papers expired three weeks ago." The man flees, and they shoot him. Uniformed Nazis, the hell beings of this realm, roam the city at will, commanded by a wrathful demon, Major Strasser (Conrad Veidt).[2] No one is above suspicion, especially the "usual suspects" rounded up regularly by the French chief of police, Captain Louis Renault (Claude Rains), in some antic attempt to convince the German authorities that something is actually being done to curb the flow of illegal immigrants through the city. What everyone wants are "letters of transit," which "cannot be questioned." These allow safe and certain passage through the multiple risks of transit. Don't we all want these—papers, documents or dogmas, sacraments or karmic merit—whatever will help us navigate our passage though the underworld and out the other side into a new birth in some heavenly realm, someplace pleasant like, say, Hollywood? And don't we all fear that our credentials will be exposed as inadequate, fake, or expired and that we will fall into the hands of the demonic, be cruelly punished, and reborn in, say, Mogadishu?

The dark prince of this transit realm is Rick (Humphrey Bogart), proprietor of the popular Café Américain. Rick has left America, the place everyone else wants to get to. It is never clear why he left, only that he cannot return. In this regard, he is a transit denizen like everyone else, except that he doesn't aspire to leave Casablanca. Rick used to be a good and honorable man; he had run guns into Ethiopia and fought with the Loyalists in Spain. He had worked and risked his life for values greater than his own self-interest. But now he is disillusioned, defending himself against lost hope with near-impregnable cynicism. He has convinced himself that nothing matters, that "I don't stick my nose out for anybody," that "I'm the only cause I'm interested in." Those around him, interestingly enough, are not taken in by Rick's attitude of cynicism. They continue to see him as a good man and know his cynicism is like the Rio Grande—a mile wide and an inch deep. We see immediately the wounded hero, played by an actor who embodied that archetype like no other—Bogie. And we sense at once that his wound is a wound of love.

He sits in his café, marinating in alcohol and resentment. His life of commitment and service has come to a bad end. He has left the field. Spiritually, Rick is a dead man walking. He has died to his previous life and cannot find his way into a favorable rebirth. What *did* happen to

Rick? What could possibly have caused him to give up the good fight? Turns out, it's still the same old story, *cherchez la femme*. His "death" happened at a Paris train station when Ilse, the woman he loved, never showed up, even as the Nazis were invading Paris in May 1940. His spirit, his faith in humanity was crushed. Her betrayal so destroyed him that he decided nothing had meaning or value.

This stance is not uncommon in contemporary culture—cynicism as a defense against a lost or disappointing faith. Values collapse. Endlessly before our eyes on television, in the movies, and in real life we see people falling apart. Naked greed for sex, money, power is the dominant theme of a culture that has lost the innate truth of its raison d'être. It is all but impossible not to lose heart, not to shut down to escape the pain. So cynicism seems the only possible stance—and it's a powerful stance. From within this fortress of disappointment and denial of meaning, it is not hard to make anyone who believes in something look like a fool—so easy that a person's spiritual evolution can get stuck here, harden up into a truly rigid cynicism. It becomes a prison of the soul, the hardest cell to break out of on one's own.

But isn't Rick's broken heart a kind of indulgence while all around him humanity's life-and-death struggle hangs in the balance? Is neutrality and withdrawal an acceptable moral stance in the face of rampant evil? If it wasn't Bogie, mightn't you want to say, "Dude, get over it. We need you." But it is Bogie, so we sympathize with how deeply he's suffering, knowing the wound of love ourselves.

The action of the film takes place late in 1941. We see Rick sign a credit slip dated December 2, 1941, just five days short of "a date which will live in infamy." Rick clearly represents isolationist America, which had refused up to then to enter the war, despite the fall of so much of Europe to the horrors of Nazism. It was one of those few cases where there is a clear right and wrong, and so much was at stake, but, like Rick, America didn't "stick its neck out for anybody." After all, over a hundred thousand Americans had fought and died in World War I, the "war to end all wars." Alas, not only did all wars not end, but nothing much changed. Like Rick, America was suffering from disillusionment and a feeling of futility, which made it turn its back on the sufferings of Europe to preoccupy itself with its own economic troubles. America had grown cynical about the common good, and had decided to stay out of the fight.

Haven't we all been there? We have lost something dear to us, and we've turned our back on all values. Suddenly nothing matters, except of course, the fact that *we* are suffering. *That* matters hugely. We feel entitled to nurture our treasured tragedy, to make our pain the central fact of our life, the pole about which we construct our identity. Who cares if the world is going up in flames? I've lost "my precious," and that is all that matters. Now we see the shallowness of our previous commitments, our lack of real will and determination, no matter how strong and unselfish we may have seemed. *Now*, we think, we have the right to quit, drown our sorrows, retreat into our castle of cynicism and sneer at the fools who still care.

But Rick gets lucky. One night at his café, "of all the gin joints in all the towns in all the world," his lost love from Paris, Ilse (Ingrid Bergman), walks in, along with her husband, Victor Laszlo (Paul Henreid), a world-famous hero of the Resistance. Ilse is as beautiful and radiant as ever, the Divine Feminine herself. She asks Rick's piano player, Sam (Dooley Wilson), to play her favorite song, "As Time Goes By." Rick hears the song, sees Ilse, and is rocked to his core. He hardly knows whether he is awake or dreaming (or, we would add, in the transit world). Naturally, he drowns his sorrows in alcohol and in a defiant, hopeless gesture orders Sam to play the song again. ("You played it for her, you can play it for me.") Later Ilse returns to the café, just as Rick knew she would, and tries to explain herself, just as he knew she would. But Rick is drunk, stuck in his disillusionment and blame. He would rather be bitter and right than hear anything else. Hurt and defeated, Ilse leaves.

Nevertheless, the Divine Feminine has begun her life-giving work. Ilse refuses to give up on Rick; she is determined to have him know the truth. Despite his cruel remarks and demeaning treatment, she perseveres. Rick slowly opens up to hearing her. He even masters his own reactivity and listens a bit as she explains why she didn't meet him at the train in Paris. When she and Rick were together there, she believed that her husband was dead. Just before she was to meet Rick at the train station, she discovered that he was still alive, and decided that her duty, her dharma, lay with Laszlo. Ilse confronts Rick on his cowardly and avoidant behavior, which he justifies by her abandonment of him. This excuse is where Rick is stuck in his transit, clinging to his past life in Paris, to his denied suffering, which he covers over with cynicism and nastiness. He feels entitled to his pain and believes it to be the one salient fact in his world. Indeed, while all around him desperate people risk their lives and their loved ones to escape from a deadly, worldwide evil, he believes his problems are the most important thing in this crazy world.

But as Rick begins honestly to show his broken heart to Ilse, his healing, his rebirth begins. He saves a young girl from forced sex with the amusingly cynical Captain Louis Renault by fixing a roulette game so that she wins enough money to save herself and her young husband. When Renault seizes on the pretext of being shocked to discover "gambling at Rick's!" to close down the café, Rick keeps everyone on salary. He is starting to work his way through his transit, slowly letting go of his fixed position of resentment and isolation. He and Ilse refind their essential love for each other, but again he comes to a fork in the road of transit. Peaceful and wrathful deities are appearing—Ilse and Laszlo, Strasser and Renault—enormously significant energies. On the one hand, Rick wants nothing more than to be with Ilse, and she is clearly willing. Their love is the love of a lifetime, as only Hollywood can portray it. On the other hand, he recognizes not only that Laszlo occupies the moral high ground, but that more is at stake here than just personal happiness. Ilse confesses her helplessness in the same dilemma. What to choose—personal happiness or moral duty? She turns the problem over to Rick and says, "You must choose for both of us."

At great personal risk, Rick outmaneuvers the tightening trap being laid by Major Strasser to jail Laszlo, and, finally, at the fog-shrouded Casablanca airport he puts Ilse on the waiting plane with Laszlo to fulfill her destined role as essential dharma partner to her husband in carrying on the work of the Resistance. Rick willingly releases Ilse into her next life in America and reclaims his own life here and now in Casablanca, so that both of them can live out their destinies. He has moved beyond personal desire into choosing the good for the benefit of all. Out of the willingness to sacrifice their personal love, Rick and Ilse find their unbreakable unity beyond space and time. Ilse says, "I said I'd never leave you," and Rick replies, "I know you never will." And in that ineffable moment, Rick acknowledges, "We'll always have Paris"— he now understands that real love exists in eternity, outside of time and space, beyond all separation or duality. It exists in the realm of Being, itself.

In this moment Rick transcends himself—he moves into a higher realm of being, one where the sense of separation opens into the feeling of oneness with all. As the Bible says, to save your life you must lose it; only in willing the good for the benefit of all can the small self, with its small-time joys and sorrows, be overcome. Personal love is always love for an object, specifically an object that makes us feel good about ourselves. It is the love of an illusion, yet we think it's supposed to heal our wounds and bring us lasting peace. This love was the way Rick had loved Ilse in Paris, and in Casablanca until almost the very end—as an object, separate from himself, whose function was to gratify him. We can see this selfish love in his immediate assumption, lived out for one and a half years in Casablanca, that Ilse's nonappearance was a betrayal, never questioning whether something had happened to her in the midst of the Nazi invasion. Only in letting go of Ilse could he love her as another being-in-herself, a person with her own destiny and path, independent of his own preferences. In that release of his personal will, Rick finds true being again: being itself *as* love, *as* compassion, being as one with itself.

Dying again, now to his false self, Rick is reborn as a committed man, transcending both idealism and cynicism. Like the heroes of most transit films, this essential self knows what must be done. His parting words to Ilse are, "I'm no good at being noble, but it doesn't take much to see that the problems of three little people don't amount to a hill of beans in this crazy world. . . . Here's looking at you, kid." The Buddhists would say Rick has entered the path of a bodhisattva, someone who is dedicated to alleviating the suffering of all beings everywhere, putting their realization before his own, even while learning that there are ultimately no others (and no self) to be saved. Laszlo acknowledges this transformation and tells Rick, "Welcome back to the fight."

And oddly enough, even as the plane takes off, Rick finds his own dharma partner, the person with whom what must be done can be done, in the unlikely person of Louis Renault, his dearest enemy/friend and fellow recovering cynic. Their partnership is based on a kind of grudging respect and a recovered commitment to the fight for the good. (Of course, Louis is not Ingrid Bergman, but, hey, if you're sensible, you work with what you're given and are grateful.) Side by side, walking ahead of us, the pair disappears into the foggy night as Rick proclaims, "Louis, I think this is the beginning of a beautiful friendship."

And two more bardo beings are born for the benefit of all. Only days later America would enter the fight for the good, prepared at last to sacrifice its own blood and treasure for the benefit of all, not in some naïve hope of a war to end all wars, but simply to do what must be done so that a freer humanity might continue its foggy, perilous, and absolutely necessary journey toward the light. All over the world people were giving up their loved ones to the wartime struggle. It was, and is, a fight for love and glory, and for a way to make those forces one.

And, as always, "The fundamental things apply, as time goes by."

Chapter Eighteen

OUR ALL-TIME FAVORITE

The Wizard of Oz

We shall not cease from exploration
And the end of all our exploring
Will be to arrive where we started
And know the place for the first time.

—T. S. Eliot

Fashionable circles of film criticism have long accepted that *Citizen Kane* is the greatest movie of all time. Times and tastes change, and it is always interesting to see what currently stands at the pinnacle.[1] We have our own list, and standing right at the top is that beloved Hollywood spectacle *The Wizard of Oz* (1939). Without brainy pretension it tells you pretty much everything needed to navigate through the transit state and emerge into everyday enlightenment—to possess what the Tibetans call "the natural mind."

The movie opens on an utterly mundane locus of life, a literal pigsty in a gray world. Dorothy, an orphan child (aren't we all, whether from loss of family or from our original source) lives on a struggling farm in Kansas with her gruff aunt and uncle and three farmhands. Her dreams and intuitions tell her there is another reality beyond this gray and limited life, and her song, "Over the Rainbow," perfectly expresses the longing for transcendence that lives as a divine spark in everyone.

Somehow, everyone dreams not so much of a static, perfect heaven but of a more colorful, meaningful, dramatic realm in which the glorious themes of love, courage, and wisdom can be played out. The song, and Judy Garland's child-into-woman demeanor and voice, deeply touch the heart and bring forth that longing for another, happier life in another dimension.

Soon Dorothy is swept out of her reality by a tornado. She journeys in her house, on her (death)bed, through swirling realms of familiar and unfamiliar images from her Kansas life. She and her house finally land in an utterly strange, yet somehow familiar country—the land of Oz. Immediately the film bursts forth into glorious Technicolor. Dorothy, understandably confused, is given a basic orientation to her situation by her benevolent transit guide, Glinda, the Good Witch of the East, who explains that Dorothy's house fell upon and killed the Wicked Witch of the South. Dorothy inherits the dead witch's magic ruby slippers, but no one seems to know how to work the magic (a problem that besets us all—we all intuitively know that somewhere within ourselves we have the answers to all our problems, but nobody tells us how to access them). Dorothy, like most recently dead people, wants only to return to the familiar, if unsatisfactory, reality she knew before. She also keenly feels her aunt's pain at her niece's loss and wants to return to Aunt Em, who was, for all her gruffness, genuinely loving. Instead, Dorothy is compelled to set out, accompanied by her little dog, Toto, another Kansan, on a journey through the magical land of Oz to find the God figure, the Wizard, who can tell her how to work the magic so she can go home. Strange but true—when confronted by the exotic and colorful novelty of Oz, all Dorothy can think to want is to return home to Kansas.

Setting out along the yellow brick road, Dorothy quickly meets three essential and lovable companions—the Scarecrow, who thinks he lacks brains, the Tin Man, who feels he has no heart, and the Cowardly Lion, who fears he is a coward, a big pussycat. Each of these figures represents a part of Dorothy's (and our) complete humanity, which we imagine ourselves to be without and long for in order to feel complete. The Lion represents the survival instinct, associated with the physical body. The Tin Man represents the relations instinct, which connects us to each other through the emotions. The Scarecrow represents the adaptation instinct, which operates through the thinking mind. Each person experiences a lack in these instincts, generally one more than the others.[2] This situation is our normal one in the bardo of this life, the transit of everyday being. Each of us is stumbling along feeling a lack and imagining that having what we lack will make us feel fulfilled. We are constantly searching outside of ourselves for the wizard with the magical cure.

Of course, on the journey toward God the adversary is never far away, and, indeed, the Wicked Witch of the West is closely observing Dorothy and company's every move, scheming to get her hands on Dorothy's ruby slippers. At one point she makes a clever move, generating a field of poppies in which Dorothy and her companions fall asleep, lost in dreams and forgetting their resolve to reach the Wizard. This sleep of forgetfulness happens to every one of us every day. We forget our intention to seek the all-important answers to life's urgent questions; we forget that life is short and death waits. Instead, we fall into our familiar everyday trances, which lull us to sleep, and we forget our true nature and ultimate purpose. Fame, money, family, sex, drugs, work, even movies seduce us into forgetting our real aims; we believe in the socially given reality without question. We forget that we seem to have come here for a purpose and that to find and fulfill that purpose is our only authentic aim.

Fortunately, however, Dorothy and her friends are not without supernatural aid of their own. Glinda, the Good Witch of the East, causes it to snow, thus destroying the effect of the poppies. They all wake up and rediscover their resolve, setting off again on the yellow brick road. Glinda (Billie Burke) is a charming figure, a kind of benevolent protector deity who embodies compassion and wisdom. Spiritual traditions hold that only the most austere souls can follow the impersonal path of direct contemplation of the formless One; most people do better when they can imagine their own inherent qualities of compassion and wisdom in a form, like that of a god or perhaps the goddess Tara, Mother Mary, or Glinda, who constantly radiates love and help to all beings without exception. However we conceptualize it, most of us sense that there are larger forces, benign and malevolent, that seem to influence our destinies. So the two witches, one helpful, the other obstructive, embody these two forces influencing the soul on its journey. In the Tibetan tradition, one meditates on one's *yidam*, the deity with whom one has the deepest relationship, as a guide and help in navigating the bardos. Ultimately, of course, we realize that even these gods and goddesses are aspects of our own true nature, which has always been one with everything.

Once Dorothy and her friends reach the Emerald City, they are frustrated by the Wizard, who first declines to see them and then refuses to help them unless they bring him the broomstick of the Wicked Witch of the West. One of the few ways in which the film failed L. Frank Baum's book was that in the book everyone was issued green glasses at the gates to the Emerald City. Everyone in the city wore green glasses, and everyone agreed that the Emerald City was indeed green. This conceit cleverly introduced the recognition that the reality each of us experiences is colored by the lenses, both individually and socially imposed, that we are wearing in any situation.

Many of us who came to the spiritual path in the 1970s had this experience, having read Baba Ram Dass's (née Richard Alpert, Harvard PhD) accounts of his transformative relationship with his guru, Neem Karoli Baba, as well as Carlos Castaneda's stories of his discipleship with the Yaqui shaman Don Juan. We were looking for our very own wizard, the one who had the answers and could help us compensate for our lacks and fulfill our longings. The wizard, we thought, would immediately see through to our soul and heal us right then and there. Well, some of us found our wizards, and they weren't too impressed with us. Mostly they told us to go out and confront our own demons and bring back real evidence of our victory. They saw how soft and naïve we were, how unprepared, for all our idealism, to cope with reality. They also saw our grandiosity, how entitled we felt to their assistance without having to put forth much effort of our own. So they sent us out into the world to deal with the witch, who wants everything we have and has a lot of power to get it.

In the film, the wicked witch's power sends out troops of flying monkeys, who swoop up Dorothy and her companions. Buddhists call the restless mind, which jumps from thought to image to memory to interpretation, the monkey mind, and thoughts can certainly seem to swoop down on us like a troop of flying monkeys and carry us off into unwanted states. Hasn't everyone had the experience of being caught up in doubt, confusion, habits, and obsessions, and lost all sense of grounding? And like those swarms of flying monkeys, thoughts always carry us back to the witch's palace, the place of maximum fear, danger, and sense of profound helplessness. Here is the archetypal testing ground of transit. Will the soul surrender to helpless fear, or will it rally in the name of love?

The movie is Hollywood Oz—was there really any doubt? When the Wicked Witch of the West lights the Scarecrow on fire, Dorothy douses his straw with her bucket of wash water, drenching the witch in the process and causing her to melt. In the instinctive act to save her friend, Dorothy unwittingly stumbles on the way to kill the witch and take her broom. Here is the open secret—that action taken from compassion is what liberates us from our dilemma of self-involvement. It is in freeing others that we are freed.

Now Dorothy has her hard-earned trophy to present to the Wizard. With true accomplishment and tested in battle, she has earned real self-respect—she can now ask directly for what she needs. The Wizard, however, seems short on answers. He blusters around until Toto, the animal spirit not impressed by reputations and wizards, pulls aside the curtain to reveal a small, noisy old guy pushing and pulling on levers and yelling into a bass microphone. The Great Wizard, it turns out, is a humbug, just another bozo from Kansas like all the rest of us. Everything we imagined about him was false, an illusion created to fool us. Imagining that he had the answers we needed was obviously naïve. It is a moment of severe disillusionment, to be sure, but this disillusionment doesn't come while the four friends are still inexperienced and unsure. They are ready to claim responsibility for their own enlightenment and to withdraw their God projections from the Wizard. Nevertheless, they are also smart enough not to reject the Wizard out of hand, and indeed it turns out that this bumbling charlatan does indeed know a trick or two. He quickly responds, in a way that intuits what each of Dorothy's companions needs to recognize his own inherent completeness. The Scarecrow receives a diploma, validating his intelligence. The Lion receives a medal for valor, allowing him to embody his already-existing and recently discovered courage. The Tin Man gets a heart-shaped testimonial watch for his incredible love and service. The three together, body, heart, and mind, are appointed the new corulers of Oz. What each one receives from the Wizard has "only" illusory value. The real gift has already been received by each one: in the time of testing each has found himself true, recognized his own wholeness, and moved beyond the sense of lack into the realm of fullness. They are ready to rule.

And in that fullness each must say goodbye to Dorothy, who is about to leave in a balloon with the Professor/Wizard. Dorothy must, in a sense, die again, this time to Oz, in order to ascend with the Wizard into the heavens. However, at the last moment Toto, the animal trickster spirit, escapes, and unable to stop the balloon, the Wizard takes off without Dorothy and Toto. Once again Dorothy's will to return home has been thwarted. At this moment Glinda reappears and informs Dorothy that she has always had the power to return home; it is only now, having achieved a balance of her own heart, mind, and body through the symbolic personae of the Scarecrow, Tin Man, and Lion that she can believe it. As she clicks the heels of her ruby slippers together and repeats, "There's no place like home," she is transported back into her bedroom in Uncle Henry and Aunt Em's Kansas farmhouse.

She awakens to find the exotic Scarecrow, Tin Man, and Lion appearing in the more ordinary guises of farmhands, and even the Wizard is there as an itinerant magician. And so Dorothy finds herself at the place where she began and knows it for the first time. Like so many of us, she'd thought that enlightenment was "over the rainbow," in some other world, with some other companions, in some other, more rarefied state of being. Instead, what she discovers is the natural mind, just as it is, resting in its own everyday empty luminosity and holy perfection. Having been consumed by fantasy, she discovers that everything she's been looking for has always been hers to have. And guess what—whether you are returning to the love and warmth of old friends and family or integrating into the universal and eternal presence of radiant luminosity, well, there truly is just no place like home.

Chapter Nineteen

ENDING UP AT SUCHNESS

I maintain that the human mystery is incredibly demeaned by scientific reductionism, with its claim in promissory materialism to account eventually for all of the spiritual world in terms of patterns of neuronal activity. This belief must be classed as a superstition. . . . We have to recognize that we are spiritual beings with souls existing in a spiritual world as well as material beings with bodies and brains existing in a material world.

—Sir John C. Eccles

We live today, for better or worse, in a largely secular culture dominated by temporal and material concerns. Skepticism is a dominant popular attitude. Faith and belief are paid lip service but considered inferior to modes of reason and logic. We vacillate in our dichotomies. But however much rationalism and scientism would like to reduce spiritual concerns to a mere defense against death anxiety, it seems that within each of us dwells an intuition of the beyond, so called because it is beyond materiality, beyond thought, beyond personality, beyond existence itself—certainly beyond anything anyone one could say about it. Most people experience this intuition quite strongly during childhood. It literally fades into the background of consciousness during adult life, during which all kind of objects, movements, and concepts capture the foreground. The foreground is often so full and so compelling that all sense of the background of awareness, within which all these events are taking place, gets lost completely. This situation is often the one in which transit film heroes find themselves at the beginning of the movie. Only when a crisis, such as contact with death, literal or psychological, pulls our attention out of its identification with the foreground does the background begin to be noticed again, now with a new urgency. The beyond, rather than everyday thoughts, feelings, and motivations, becomes the dominant reality.

In writing this book, we use rather neutral terms like *beyond* and *unity,* or even *the One,* rather than a more specifically religious one like *God.* As to that, there is a natural variance among humans. Some intuit the Divine, the One, as a person, a pure conscious Being that contains and transcends everything; that person is the Beloved, and one's impulse is to unite with it in love. Others, having the same intuition of the unity of all, interpret their realization as the experience of a vast, all embracing flow, both profoundly good and utterly impersonal. They are nontheists, and their ranks include Buddhists. Of course, if both theists and nontheists are having an authentic intuition of the One, they're both experiencing the same One. All rivers flow to the ocean.

So these two primordial themes—the crisis of death and an intuition of the transcendent—are what drive the transit film. It is a form that always starts, in a sense, where Dante started, alone "in the middle of the journey of our life."[1] It gives us a man or woman who has come to the end of the road: face to face with death, certainly with the death of all that person values and holds dear and, ultimately, with physical/mental death itself. This encounter can be a place of terror. Standing alone, "There is *nothing* the separate self can *do* to *actually* get rid of death terror, since the separate self *is* that death terror—they come into existence together and they only disappear together."[2]

Addressing exactly that pain and suffering, the Buddha himself gave us the Four Noble Truths:

1) the truth of suffering

2) the truth of its origin

3) the truth of its cessation

4) the truth of the path which leads to that cessation[3]

As pointed out by the Dalai Lama, the causes of suffering within ourselves must be acknowledged, understood, and eliminated, and the path to suffering's complete cessation must be engaged. We have attempted to illustrate in any number of the transit films evoked in this book that one does not consciously engage in such a path without accepting what Achaan Chah tells us is the second form of suffering: the suffering that leads to the end of suffering (chapter 3). As expressed by Mahayana Buddhism's most beloved Heart Sutra, we must go beyond our suffering.

Gate/Gate/Paragate
Parasam gate
Bodhi Svaha

Gone/Gone/Gone Beyond
Utterly Beyond
Oh what an awakening[4]

Transit films take one beyond but seldom end in a clouds-and-angels heaven. Usually the protagonists either return to human life (seldom in an infant form) with a deeper understanding and a new sense of both acceptance and purpose, or they go on to what they sense is a new set of tasks and challenges in other realms of creation. Transit films seem to demonstrate, over and over, that the crisis of death can produce spiritual transformation. They further say that transformation need not take place in linear time—it can take place in a cinematic second or in the dimension of timelessness. Transit films strongly suggest that death is more like an opportunity for promotion (or demotion) than a heartless finality. There is, by convention, a struggle of sorts, an internal battle with one's own demons, a recollection or reconnection to what is most essential within one's self, something innately experienced as *not* alone, *not* separate—call it what you will: the Divine Spark, the Guru within, Enlightenment, Connection, Unity, Destiny, Wisdom, Oneness, Grace, Love, or, quite simply, Suchness. Whatever we say about it is a creation of the human mind. The Indian mystic known as Rajneesh said it well: "Existence is a mystery, and one should accept it as a mystery and not pretend to have any explanation. No, explanation is not needed— only exclamation, a wondering heart, awakened, surprised, feeling the mystery of life each moment. Then, and only then, you know what truth is. And truth liberates."[5]

That—and a good movie!

Friend, hope for the Guest while you are alive.
Jump into experience while you are alive!
Think . . . and think . . . while you are alive.
What you call "salvation" belongs to the time before death.

If you don't break your ropes while you're alive,
do you think
ghosts will do it after?

The idea that the soul will join with the ecstatic
just because the body is rotten —
that is all fantasy.
What is found now is found then.
If you find nothing now,
you will simply end up with an apartment in the City of Death.
If you make love with the divine now, in the next life
        you will have the face of satisfied desire.

So plunge into the truth, find out who the Teacher is,
        Believe in the Great Sound!

Kabir says this: When the Guest is being searched for,
        it is the intensity of the longing for the Guest
        that does all the work.
Look at me, and you will see a slave of that intensity.

—Kabir[6]

ACKNOWLEDGMENTS

Our root teacher, Oscar Ichazo, once said that there are really only four gratitiudes: for the creation, for humanity, for all those who have taken humanity to true enlightenment, and for the guidance we receive from the School (the big School of Wisdom from which all true traditions derive). Nevertheless, we cannot resist offering our gratitude to these people:

Oscar Ichazo, founder of the Arica School, who set our feet on the wisdom path, and who told us that "box office is *vox dei.*"

Jack Downing, MD, whose love, encouragement, and all-around crazy wisdom made me a real therapist.

Jack Lee Rosenberg, PhD, who taught me to "follow the aliveness."

Richard Miller, PhD, dear friend and teacher.

Glen Gabbard, MD, whose book *The Movies on Your Mind* first opened us to the connection between film and psychology.

Blessed Esalen Institute in Big Sur, where the renaissance of consciousness came to flower.

My clients, whose courage and deep aspiration move me every day.

And to all our brothers and sisters in the School, who have accompanied us on this journey all these years.

—Lyn Genelli

Oscar, friend and teacher, who pointed the way to an innate awareness, of clarity upon emptiness.

ACKNOWLEDGMENTS

His Holiness the Dalai Lama, Pema Chödrön, Namkhai Norbu, Francesca Freemantle, and Sogyal Rinpoche for their written wisdom.

Pauline Kael, Ed Landberg, and William K. Everson, who forged my knowledge and appreciation of motion pictures.

Peter L. Valenti for his love of film blanc.

Turner Classic Movies, whose regular programming of almost every film in our book was a truly valuable asset.

The good people at Quest Books who guided us through the labyrinth of publication: Richard Smoley; Sharron Dorr; Jessica Salasek; our permissions editor, Sheri Gilbert; and our editor, Will Marsh, who magically made it appear that I could write something readable.

Finally, to all those who in one way or another have supported us in the writing of this book: Everett Aison, Mary Jane Anthony, Tim Curnen, Syd Dutton, Christian Intemann, Amy Lenzo, Richard Starbuck Maxwell, Polly Osborne, Jackie Clair Wood, and Rudy Wurlitzer.

—Tom Genelli

All in this book that is true, relevant, or useful we owe entirely to the wisdom and grace of our teachers. All errors, misinterpretations and stupidities are ours alone.

NOTES

INTRODUCTION

1. *Outward Bound*, with its opening credits, quickly offers a disclaimer of any intent to offend viewers' religious convictions. In explaining the studio's anxiety about public reaction to the film's subject, Andrew Sarris noted that *Outward Bound* "tended to institutionalize passage into the next world in terms of a well-ordered ocean liner drifting to an unknown destination, a *Twilight Zone* long before its time" ("The Afterlife, Hollywood Style," *American Film* 4, no. 6 [April 1979]: 25).

   Sarris, at once insightful, informative, inspired, intelligent, and irreverent, died as we were completing this book. His well-considered observation from the introduction to *You Ain't Heard Nothin' Yet* (New York: Oxford University Press, 1998) is as pertinent today as when written and is quoted with the highest respect: "There is absolutely nothing wrong with the practice of belles-lettres in the writing of film history as long as belles-lettres contents itself with commenting on cinema, and does not presume to impersonate it. The gap between movies and the words used to describe them must always be understood between the writer and the reader. And it must be understood also that there can be no equivalent in even the most illuminating literary fireworks for the *son et lumiere* that makes up the essential experience of the sound film."

2. Peter L. Valenti, "The Film *Blanc*: Suggestions for a Variety of Fantasy, 1940–45," *Journal of Popular Film* 4, no. 4 (1978): 294–303.

3. "The dead were expected to participate in the institutions of social life in Egypt, either within religious rituals or in the journey to the afterlife, in which such scenes as judgment recapitulated the values of Egyptian

culture. . . . The notion of a consistent 'self' was reached in parallel fashion with the development of the notion of a transcendent *akh*, the glorified body of the afterlife. . . . As more and more people were able to attain to the *akh* state, however, a judgment scene developed in Egyptian literature. . . . The idea appeared that a person's destiny depends upon the absence of complaints made against him or his ability to refute them in the heavenly court. . . . The emphasis of the judgment shifts to the person's own moral achievement" (Alan F. Segal, *Life After Death: A History of the Afterlife in Western Religion* [New York: Doubleday, 2004], 52–53, 56).

The films *Between Two Worlds, A Matter of Life and Death*, and *Defending Your Life* provide interesting tableaux of justice in afterlife courts.

4. The word *transit* is generally used to denote one's passing from the living realm to what is beyond. While many Buddhists and writers about Buddhism use the word *transit* for that purpose, the writer E. J. Gold was among the earliest Americans to equate transit with the teachings of *The Tibetan Book of the Dead* in describing a uniquely nonpsychedelic, experiential, homegrown variation of that book's teachings (*American Book of the Dead* [San Francisco: And/Or Press, 1975]).

5. The potential of such an understanding is explored and described in the works of the philosopher and metaphysician Oscar Ichazo, Arica Institute, Inc. (http:www.arica.org/), and in the Buddhist study *Self Realization Through Seeing with Naked Awareness*, translation and commentary by John Myrdhin Reynolds, foreword by Namkhai Norbu (Ithaca, NY: Snow Lion Publications, 2000).

CHAPTER ONE

Epigraph. *What Is Life?* (Cambridge: Cambridge University Press, 1944), 89.

1. Valenti, "Film *Blanc*," 295 (see introduction, n. 2).
2. Siegfried Kracauer, *Theory of Film* (London: Oxford University Press, 1960).

CHAPTER TWO

Epigraph. BrainyQuote,
   http://www.brainyquote.com/quotes/quotes/i/isaacasimo103611.html.

1. Valenti, "Film *Blanc*," 295 (see introduction, n. 2).
2. Throughout the remainder of the text the terms *bardo* and *transit* are used interchangeably. The religion/philosophy of Buddhism comprises many differing sects and schools within sects. (Wikipedia has an excellent analysis of the distinction between the various vehicles and forms of Buddhism.) Material regarding the bardo explored in this book is primarily derived from the Tibetan Vajrayana ("the indestructible way") tradition, a school of Tantric Buddhism. The Vajrayana school has possibly had the widest impact on American culture's relationship to Buddhism in the past forty years, equaling the interest in Zen practice and other schools of Buddhism—strong measures for difficult times. We reference three specific translations when discussing the texts of *The Tibetan Book of the Dead*:

   - *The Tibetan Book of the Dead, or The After-Death Experience on the Bardo Plane, according to Lama Kazi Dawa-Samdup's English Rendering*, compiled and edited by W. Y. Evans-Wentz, with a psychological commentary by C. G. Jung (London: Oxford Univeristy Press, 1927);
   - *The Tibetan Book of the Dead: The Great Liberation Through Hearing in the Bardo*, Shambala, trans. with commentary by Francesca Fremantle and Chögyam Trungpa (Berkeley: Shambala, 1975);
   - Francesca Fremantle, *Luminous Emptiness: Understanding the Tibetan Book of the Dead* (Boston: Shambala, 2001).

   Fremantle points out that while *The Tibetan Book of the Dead* is used and respected by all the schools of Tibetan Buddhism, it is so especially in the Nyingma and Kagyu traditions. Generally the various Tibetan Buddhist traditions accept the after-death state of bardo, or transit, as one of the natural states of existence—birth, life, death, and transit. They define bardo as a condition of uncertainty, a state of existing between death and rebirth within which consciousness travels, experiencing the unwinding of the mind and the projections of all that has seduced and scarred the psyche during its lifetime. The word *bardo* can literally be translated as "gap," a space or state that lies between two other states. In reading from a variety of texts explaining the bardo, it is clear that there are variations among different traditions and schools, particularly in nomenclature, but that there is general agreement on the overall principles.

In her brilliant 2001 follow-up commentary, *Luminous Emptiness: Understanding the Tibetan Book of the Dead*, Fremantle explains that while originally the term *bardo* referred only to that specific period between one life and the next, "Later Buddhism expanded the whole concept to distinguish six or more similar states, covering the whole cycle of life, death, and rebirth" (54). She defines the six bardos as the bardo of this life ("the condition of life into which we are born"); the bardo of dream; the bardo of meditation; the bardo of dying; the bardo of *dharmata* ("the essential quality of reality"); and the bardo of existence (or becoming). The bardo of dream and the bardo of meditation both take place in the bardo of this life. "Wherever there is the death of one state of mind, there is the birth of another, and linking the two there is bardo" (55).

Such distinctions became increasingly relevant in transit films made in the late 1980s and after, informed as they were by more accessible Buddhist teachings, teachers, and texts—films such as *Jacob's Ladder* (1990), *Ghost* (1990), *Groundhog Day* (1993), *The Sixth Sense* (1999), *Birth* (2004), and *Hereafter* (2010).

3. Valenti, "Film *Blanc*," 302.
4. Sarris, "The Afterlife, Hollywood Style," 26 (see introduction, n. 1).

CHAPTER THREE

Epigraph. *The Tibetan Yoga of Dream and Sleep* (Ithaca, NY: Snow Lion Publications, 1998), 26.

1. The Buddhist concept of emptiness (*shunyata*) refers to the emptiness of inherent, independent existence. It is a subtle concept, open to much misinterpretation. In the words of Robert F. Thurman, "Voidness does not mean nothingness, but rather that all things lack intrinsic reality, intrinsic objectivity, intrinsic identity or intrinsic referentiality. Lacking such static essence or substance does not make them not exist—it makes them thoroughly relative" (foreword to Lex Hixon, *Mother of the Buddhas: Meditation on the Prajnaparamita Sutra* [Wheaton, IL: Quest Books,1993], xvii).

   In his book *The Universe in a Single Atom* (New York: Morgan Road Books, 2005), the Dalai Lama refers to the theory of emptiness as one of the most important philosophical insights in Buddhism. His cogent remarks can be read at http://en.wikipedia.org/wiki/Emptiness_(Buddhism).

2. The second kind of suffering is often referred to as conscious suffering. The mystic Gurdjieff referred to it as intentional suffering. Its essential quality is that the pain of one's suffering is not projected outward and onto others but is accepted and processed internally as part of one's path toward self-realization.

   The Gelug/Kagyu Tradition of Mahamudra by His Holiness The Dalai Lama and Alexander Berzin (Ithaca, NY: Snow Lion Publications, 1997) is an excellent study examining systems of meditation on both the conventional and ultimate natures of mind, and the nonduality of subject and object. Chapters 4 and 5 are particularly germane to the topic of innate ignorance.

   Over two thousand years ago the Indian sage Patanjali defined ignorance as false identification, a misunderstanding of one's real nature. "The central act of ignorance is the identification of the Atman, which is consciousness itself, with the mind-body—'that which merely reflects consciousness.' This is what Patanjali defines as egoism" (*How to Know God: The Yoga Aphorisms of Patanjali* [Hollywood, CA: Vedanta Press, 1981], 113).

Buddhism, as its basis, follows the recorded teachings of Gautama Buddha, the essential one being that suffering is inseparable from existence. It posits that our fusion or identification with what we conventionally perceive as internal and external reality keeps us in a state of innate ignorance. Inward extinction of that identification can free the self and the senses and culminate in a state of illumination beyond both suffering and existence. Both Tantric Buddhists and the practitioners of Western wisdom schools might advocate the development, through meditation and other practices, of discriminating wisdom, a beginning of objective apprehension that recognizes and embraces the inevitability of impermanence and death and an elimination of aggression and fear due to ignorance of their true nature and place in the larger scheme of being.

3. Morris Dickstein, "It's A Wonderful Life, But . . . ," *American Film* 5, no. 7 (May 1980): 43.

4. Ibid., 47.

5. Outside Valenti's time frame but worthy of comment is the very curious *Peter Ibbetson* (1935), starring Gary Cooper and Ann Harding as aging childhood sweethearts doomed throughout their lives to be kept apart. Although they are unable to be together physically, the intensity of their bond manifests as an ability to join together each night in the sharing of a mutual dream state. The film suggests that this shared experience of union will become permanent at death. The particular realm they share is the bardo of dream, and for Buddhist practitioners this bardo can be a powerful method of reinforcing in oneself a realization of the illusory, impermanent nature of what we conventionally take as rock-solid reality. While this realization is basic to working with any of the bardos, it is said to be "particularly necessary preparation for working with dreams, because dreams arise from karmic traces deeply imprinted in the mind, and so they are very hard to influence directly. Only after our intense attachment to our ordinary concept of reality is loosened does it become

possible to perceive the world of dream, too, as our own creation and to control it" (Fremantle, *Luminous Emptiness*, 62 [see chap. 2, n. 2]). This degree of working with the dream state is, of course, hardly to be found in *Peter Ibbetson*, but the film presents the seeds of future bardo realms to be explored.

6. A more contemporary version of the transit realm is found in Albert Brooks's 1991 comedy *Defending Your Life*—an IBM-inspired model of transit, perfectly organized, pastel-colored corporate settings where everything runs with total efficiency, from the top right on down to the vapid, deluxe chain hotels where departed souls stay until they go before judgment committees to defend the lives they have lived and be assigned to their just and appropriate destiny.

    Perhaps filmdom's most bizarre vision of transit can found in Tim Burton's 1988 surreal comedy *Beetlejuice*, in which a deceased couple's efforts to cope with transit are guided by a caseworker at the Waiting Room for Lost Souls who recommends they follow the instructions in their copy of *The Handbook for the Recently Deceased*. We offer the opinion that the most easily accessible approximation to a bardo experience is to be had in air travel, especially when waiting in terminals at night between long flights.

7. *The Catechism of the Catholic Church* (United States Catholic Conference, Inc., 1994), 1473.

8. Ibid., 1472.

9. Audience of August 4, 1999, www.vatican.va/holy_father/john_paul_ii/ audiences/1999/documents/hf.

CHAPTER FOUR

1. Sarris, "The Afterlife, Hollywood Style," 25 (see introduction, n. 1).

2. Timothy Leary, Ralph Metzner, and Richard Alpert, *The Psychedelic Experience* (New Hyde Park, NY: University Books and Citadel Press, 1964).

3. Evans-Wentz, *Tibetan Book of the Dead* (see chap. 2, n. 2).

4. Iven Lourie, editor's foreword to E. J. Gold, *American Book of the Dead*, 30th Anniversary Edition (Nevada City, CA: Gateways/IDHHB, 2005), xiii.

5. Raymond Moody, *Reflections on Life After Life* (Harrisburg, PA: Stackpole Books, 1977); Robert A. Monroe, *Journeys Out of the Body* (Garden City, NY: Doubleday, 1971); Elisabeth Kübler-Ross, *On Death & Dying* (New York: Simon & Schuster/Touchstone, 1969); *Death: The Final Stage of Growth* (New York: Simon & Schuster/Touchstone, 1974).

6. Fremantle and Trungpa, *Tibetan Book of the Dead* (see chap. 2, n. 2).

7. Ibid., xi.

8. Sogyal Rinpoche, *The Tibetan Book of Living and Dying*, ed. Patrick Gaffney and Andrew Harvey (New York: Harper San Francisco, 1992), 11.

9. "The pure luminosity of the dharmata is shining before you; recognize it. . . . At this moment your state of mind is by nature pure emptiness. . . . This is the dharmata, the female buddha Samantabhadri. But this state of mind is not just blank emptiness, it is unobstructed, sparkling, pure and vibrant; this mind is the male buddha Samantabhadra. These two, your mind whose nature is emptiness without any substance whatever, and your mind which is vibrant and luminous, are inseparable; this is the dharmakaya of the buddha. This mind of yours is inseparable luminosity and emptiness in the form of a great mass of light, it has no birth or death; therefore it is the buddha of Immortal Light. To recognize this is all that is necessary. When you recognize this pure nature of your mind as the buddha, looking into your own mind is resting in the buddhamind" (Fremantle and Trungpa, *Tibetan Book of the Dead*, 37).

10. Ibid., 2. Fremantle's proposition that the transit experience is part of our basic psychological makeup is exquisitely realized in John Boulting's complex and intelligent 1942 film *Thunder Rock*. Not quite falling under Peter Valenti's conventions for the film blanc, and based on an anti-isolationist play by Robert Ardrey, it tells the story of a British journalist and war correspondent (Michael Redgrave) whose warnings about the impending onslaught of fascism are ignored to such a degree that he retreats into cynicism and despair, isolating himself as a lighthouse

keeper on Lake Michigan. There his interior life becomes peopled by the ghosts of European immigrant passengers drowned in a shipwreck almost a century before. While he functions efficiently in his role as light-keeper, his imagination engages in conversations and debates with the dead victims of the shipwreck. His conscience, in the form of the ship's dead captain, eventually leads him to a more compassionate perspective and humanely productive position, allowing him to recommit to humanity's struggle against fascism.

11. John C Lilly, foreword to *American Book of the Dead*, revised ed. (San Francisco: And/Or Press, 1975), inside cover.

12. "No topic has occupied American discussions of the afterlife as much as Near Death Experiences (NDEs), which have a number of common themes beyond the fearful emergencies that cause them—bright light, a feeling of warmth, a long tunnel, a meeting with deceased family members, a reluctant return to painful existence. Those who experienced them usually find their faith strengthened or confirmed, and left the American public significantly impressed" (Segal, *Life after Death*, 14 [see introduction, n. 3]). *Resurrection* and *Hereafter* offer standard Hollywood renditions of popularly accepted reports of NDEs.

As if to reinforce the above comments, even as we were editing this book the two best-selling books in the country were *Heaven is for Real*, by Lynn Vincent, and *Proof of Heaven*, by Eben Alexander, M.D., both elaborate descriptions of near-death experiences. Alexander, a highly respected academic neurosurgeon, describes his experiences while in a weeklong coma after contracting bacterial meningitis. In an appendix to the book, he offers a number of neuroscientific hypotheses he considered to explain his experience of being in heaven during his coma. He ends the book by saying that, for him, his experiences "break the back of the last efforts of reductive science to tell the world that the material realm is all that exists, and that consciousness, or spirit—yours and mine—is not the great and central mystery of the universe. I'm living proof" (*Proof of Heaven: A Neurosurgeon's Journey into the Afterlife* [New York: Simon & Schuster, 2012], 171).

CHAPTER FIVE

Epigraph. Sogyal Rinpoche, *Tibetan Book of Living and Dying*, 104 (see chap. 4, n. 8).

1. This quote is a variation of a quote by the British geneticist, J. B. S. Haldane (1892–1964): "Now my own suspicion is that the universe is not only queerer than we suppose, but queerer than we *can* suppose" (*Possible Worlds and Other Papers* [New York: Harper and Brothers, 1927], 286; found at http://en.wikiquote.org/wiki/J._B._S._Haldane).

2. Dzigar Kongtrül, *It's Up to You* (Boston and London: Shambhala, 2005), 6.

3. Ken Wilber, *Eye to Eye: The Quest for a New Paradigm* (Garden City, NY: Anchor Press, 1983), 73.

4. Evans-Wentz, *Tibetan Book of the Dead*, xxxvii (see chap. 2, n. 2).

5. Norman K. Dorn, "A Bit of Chicanery Led to a Brilliant Directing Career," *San Francisco Chronicle*, December 5, 1982. Cultural critic and social analyst Neal Gabler declared *It's A Wonderful Life* to be Capra's most extraordinary film, writing that Capra "propounded what one could call a theology of comedy—a secularized displacement of Christ's tale in which a common-man hero, blessed with goodness and sense, overcomes obstacles, temptations, and even betrayals to redeem his own life and triumph. . . . The hero actually attempts suicide and is 'resurrected' by divine intervention. . . . Capra (in his body of work) also created a powerful myth for the nation—one that would help sustain and define Americans for decades. 'The ecumenical church of humanism,' he called it. Others called it simply 'being an American'" (*An Empire of Their Own: How the Jews Invented Hollywood* [New York: Anchor Books, 1989], 173).

CHAPTER SIX

Epigraph. Freemantle, *Luminous Emptiness*, 234 (see chap. 2, n. 2).

1. Following Francesca Fremantle's bardo schemata, three bardos, occurring sequentially, address the overall process of dying—the bardo of dying in which occurs the actual bodily process of dying; the bardo of dharmata in which is experienced the peaceful and wrathful deities; and the bardo of existence that can determine either liberation or rebirth. Jacob clearly experiences all three.

2. The subplot of "the Ladder" as a secret experimental drug utilized by the military in Vietnam seems very like what screenwriter Angus McPhail termed a MacGuffin, a device Alfred Hitchcock famously adapted and used throughout his career. Its utility is as a deliberately mysterious plot pretext that is neither relevant nor important: it simply keeps the story going. One can readily see why a MacGuffin might be handy in a film whose core plot is primarily a cinematic visualization of a sacred Buddhist text dealing with transit, in this case the bardo of dying. In what seems an attempt to reduce audience confusion, the studio included a scene and even tacked a textual disclaimer onto the end of the movie basically stating that the reason the film might seem strange was because it was about an experimental drug, the Ladder, tested in the field on American servicemen in Vietnam.

3. *Jacob's Ladder*, manifestly a film about the bardo of dying, temporally occurs during the dissolution of Jacob's life from the time of his wounding to his last breath. His experiences are an unwinding and resolution of his karma, the chain of cause and effect linking past, present, and future. We experience Jake's experience in the real time of the movie, neither more nor less.

CHAPTER SEVEN

Epigraph. Sri Nisargadatta Maharaj, *I Am That* (Durham, NC: The Acorn Press, 1997), 8.

1. William Wordsworth, "Intimations of Immortality from Recollections of Early Childhood," stanza 5.
2. Wilber, *Eye to Eye*, 201–46 (see chap. 5, n. 3).

CHAPTER EIGHT

Epigraph. *The Essential Rumi*, trans. Coleman Barks with John Moyne, A. J. Arberry, and Reynold Nicholson (Edison, NJ: Castle Books, 1997), 281.

1. Judy Tatelbaum, *The Courage to Grieve: Creative Living, Recovery and Growth though Grief* (New York: Harper & Row, 1980), 9.
2. Sogyal Rinpoche, *Tibetan Book of Living and Dying*, 299 (see chap. 4, n. 8).
3. Ibid., 303.
4. Ibid., 46.
5. Dale Borglum, "The Beloved Can Only Be Everything," *Living/Dying Project Newsletter*, Winter 2012, 1.

CHAPTER NINE

Epigraph. Ken Wilber, *Up From Eden* (Boulder, CO: Shambhala, 1981), 57.

1. Albert Lawrence Brooks, an actor, writer, comedian, and film director born in Beverly Hills to a singer/actress mother and a radio comedian father, cut his professional teeth in stand-up comedy clubs and cutthroat competitive television. Wikipedia's keen assessment of his onstage persona, "that of an egotistical, narcissistic, nervous comic, an ironic showbiz insider who punctured himself before an audience by assembling his mastery of comedic stage craft," is realized fully in *Defending Your Life*.

NOTES

2. Segal, *Life after Death*, 714 (see introduction, n.1).

3. Belief in reincarnation is an ancient phenomenon, a central tenet of the ancient Indian religious traditions such as Hinduism, Jainism, and Sikhism. The doctrine was subscribed to by a number of early Greek philosophers as well. The Buddhist notion of rebirth differs from those earlier traditions in that there is no "self" or eternal soul to reincarnate; there is no transmigration in the strict sense.

    Buddhism does not reject the process of rebirth, but suggests that it occurs across five or six realms of being. A major diaspora of Buddhist and Hindu teachers and teachings to the West in the1960s and '70s led to significant numbers of people developing a belief in reincarnation, as well as the production of a number of books, films, and television series. The Internet Movie Database (IMDb) lists 266 movies on the subject.

4. Wilber, *Up From Eden*, 58.

5. Sri Nisargadatta Maharaj, *I Am That*, 204 (see chap. 7, epigraph).

6. Wilber, *Up From Eden*, 59.

7. Alice A. Bailey writes in her commentary on *The Yoga Sutras of Patanjali*: "The akashic record is like an immense photographic film, registering all the desires and earth experiences of our planet. Those who perceive it will see pictured thereon:

    1. The life experiences of every human being since time began,

    2. The reactions to experience of the entire animal kingdom,

    3. The aggregation of the thought-forms of a karmic nature (based on desire) of every human unit throughout time. Herein lies the great deception of the records. Only a trained occultist can distinguish between actual experience and those astral pictures created by imagination and keen desire" (*Light of the Soul: Its Science and Effects—A Paraphrase of The Yoga Sutras of Patanjali* [New York: Lucis Publishing Company, 1927], 276).

8. Wilber, *Up from Eden*, 59.

CHAPTER TEN

Epigraph: Quoted in Jack Kornfield, *After the Ecstasy, the Laundry: How the Heart Grows Wise on the Spiritual Path* (New York: Bantam, 2001), 295.

1. Fremantle, *Luminous Emptiness*, 68 (see chap. 2, n. 2).
2. Sir Walter Scott, *The Lay of the Last Minstrel*, canto 6, stanza 1.
3. The history of both Eastern and Western philosophy reflects humanity's attempts to come to terms with our basic existential issues. Over twenty-five hundred years ago the Hindu philosophical system Sankhya asserted that suffering results from our confusion of the ever-changing with the unchanging—the seen with the seer. Failure to distinguish between the two leads directly to suffering. Later, Advaita recognized that the "seen" is not actually an independent or solid entity, but is instead maya, illusion, a mere projection of our everyday mind. Later, Buddhism would refer to this mind as the conventional mind, the mind of concepts and language. The source of the conventional mind is awareness (Sanskrit *vidya*), the deepest nature of mind, its voidness and absence of existing in any fantasized, impossible way. Tantra (both Indian and Buddhist) states that the seen, the conventional, is not quite either real or unreal. It's unreal in that it has no absolute existence, but it's real in that it exists—the "seen" actually *is* the reflection of the "seer"—the two are not separate. Buddhists refer to these two minds as the absolute mind and the conventional or relative mind, saying that with intrinsic awareness, unclouded by our judgments and conceptual structures, we can recognize that our true consciousness is in everything, and that everything is part of the one eternal void. In a sense, it might be said that the whole phenomenal world exists only so that consciousness may recognize itself. This "self" is not anything that can conventionally be considered "me"—the sum total of my physical, emotional, and mental being encapsulated into what we refer to as personality. In fact, such a view could be defined by Buddhists as a central act of ignorance, the

false identification of consciousness itself with the mind/body—that which merely reflects consciousness.

4. In his book *Dzogchen: The Self Perfected State*, Chögyal Namkhai Norbu writes, "From our limited point of view, we can get discouraged thinking that to purify our karma will take many lifetimes. . . . But karma is not in fact a material accumulation, and does not depend upon externals; rather its power to condition us depends on the obstacles that impede our knowledge. If we compare our karma and the ignorance that creates it to a dark room, knowledge of the primordial state would be like a lamp, which, when lit in the room, at once causes the darkness to disappear, enlightening everything. In the same way, if one has the presence of the primordial state, one can overcome all hindrances in an instant" (ed. Adriano Clemente, trans. John Shane [London: Arkana, 1989], 40).

5. Pema Chödrön, *The Wisdom of No Escape and the Path of Loving Kindness* (Boston: Shambhala, 2010).

6. Kongtrül, *It's Up to You*, 63n (see chap. 5, n. 2).

7. Jack Kornfield, *A Path with Heart: A Guide Through the Perils and Promises of Spiritual Life* (New York: Bantam Books, 1993), 88.

CHAPTER ELEVEN

Epigraph: Hee-jin Kim, *Eihei Dogen, Mystical Realist* (Somerville, MA: Wisdom Publications, 2004), xxiv.

1. Made while the world was at war, and dealing with the gravest of subjects—death and transit—the early 1940s films blanc were still able to capture that most delicate and delightful of qualities, charm. So many of them managed to possess what was referred to in those days as "the Lubitsch touch"—director Ernst Lubitsch's unerring ability to convey through his actors the joy and humor of outrageous and/or dangerous situations that are resolved in the most charming fashion. A perfect example is Jack Benny's role as Gestapo Colonel Ehrhardt in Lubitsch's comedy *To Be or Not to Be* (1943). When considering the body of film blanc, one quickly

recognizes Lubitsch's influence on so many of them—*Here Comes Mr. Jordan, A Guy Named Joe, Angel on My Shoulder, A Matter of Life and Death, It's a Wonderful Life, The Ghost and Mrs. Muir, The Bishop's Wife*— each glowing with such charm that we are pleased, soothed, and delighted to the degree that we are fully enchanted. Such a gift!

CHAPTER TWELVE

Epigraph. Jack Kornfield and Paul Breiter, compilers, *A Still Forest Pool: The Insight Meditation of Achaan Chah* (Wheaton, IL: Quest Books, 1985), 33.

1. "In Marx's dark vision, the consistent element was that only human labor could provide surplus value, but with ruthless consequences. This is why Marx, never shy of the provocative metaphor, compared the capitalist class to the undead, because vampire-like, it only lives by sucking living labor" (Alan Briskin, *Becoming Conscious of Capitalism: The Death and Rebirth of Prosperity's Dream*, a serial narrative, www.thepowerofourcollectivewisdom.com).

CHAPTER THIRTEEN

Epigraph. Freemantle, *Luminous Emptiness*, 6 (see chap. 2, n. 2).

1. To heal the Fisher King, the keeper of the Holy Grail, the knight Percival must ask him the right question, "Whom does the Grail serve?" Percival's failure to do so leads to the kingdom becoming a wasteland.
2. "In the Buddhist philosophical world, the concept of time as relative is not alien. Before the second century c.e., the Sautrantika school argued against the notion of time as absolute. Dividing the temporal process into the past, present, and future, the Sautrantikas demonstrated the interdependence of the three and argued for the untenability of any notion of independently real past, present, and future. They showed that time cannot be conceived as an intrinsically real entity existing independently

of temporal phenomena but must be understood as a set of relations among temporal phenomena. Apart from the temporal phenomena upon which we construct the concept of time, there is no real time that is somehow the grand vessel in which things and events occur, an absolute that has an existence of its own" (Dalai Lama, *Universe in a Single Atom*, 60 [see chap. 3, n. 1]).

CHAPTER FOURTEEN

Epigraph. Lex Hixon, *Mother of the Buddhas: Meditation on the Prajnaparamita Sutra* (Wheaton, IL: Quest Books, 1993), 248.

1. "In the Greek understanding, the three highest measures of value were the Good, the True, and the Beautiful. In the final analysis all three of these were taken to be objective in character. In the most exalted vision, such as Plato's, it is proposed that all three ultimately have the same foundation. For Plato one arrives at truth by analogy in philosophy and by ratios in mathematics. One arrives at the good by finding the right point between two extremes. Beauty is a matter of grace, harmony, and proportion. The right proportion, the Golden Mean, is equally applicable in arriving at truth, goodness, or beauty. Neither the True, nor the Good, nor the Beautiful depends in any way on the inquirer; all three of these highest categories are built into the nature and being of the universe" (Marion Deckert, *The Artist As Hero*, www.icinet.org/pub/facdialogue/25/decker25).

2. Paul Brians, et al., eds., *Reading About the World*, vol. 1 (Fort Worth, TX: Harcourt Brace Custom Publishing, 1999). This notion that truth is embedded in our consciousness was a concept of central importance to the Greek philosophers and was called *anamnesis*, a calling to mind, a remembrance, or a recollection. What was essentially recollected was the eternal presence within of an innate knowledge of the Good, the True, and the Beautiful, a blessed trinity experienced as one unified comprehension of the very ground of being.

3. In his excellent article "Previews of a Call for Change" (Ask Mick LaSalle, *San Francisco Chronicle Datebook*, December 14, 2008), film reviewer Mick LaSalle suggests that the enormous box-office support provided by the fourteen-to-twenty-four-year-old market for horror, terror, and mad-slasher movies is fed by a deeply psychological need for an experiential process that challenges our capacity to endure and prevail over even the most horrific imaginings and events up to and including our own annihilation and what lies beyond, in a sense surviving our most frightening fantasies. We agree, and observe that in a culture that provides its young with little or no meaningful initiations into deeper levels of self-awareness, young people have adopted their own—an initiation of violence for violent times. The most vivid current examples of this trend are embodied in the series of films titled *Final Destination* and *Saw*.

4. Dalai Lama, *Universe in a Single Atom*, 137 (see chap. 3, n. 1).

CHAPTER FIFTEEN

Epigraph. Sogyal Rinpoche, *Tibetan Book of Living and Dying*, 50 (see chap. 4, n. 8).

1. This scene was vigorously booed at the Venice Film Festival by a strongly disapproving audience. The words "child pornography" were used. Some critics have offered this incident as the reason for the film's lukewarm reception in the United States, but it's also possible that the film's excruciating ambiguity can take the credit for that.

2. This tale is told to Lauren Bacall and Lionel Barrymore by Humphrey Bogart in the 1948 film *Key Largo*, directed by John Huston. Thinking about Bacall and Danny Huston (who is John's son) in *Birth* provides a wonderful degrees-of-separation moment.

3. Sheila Johnston, "Giving *Birth* to a Scandal," London *Daily Telegraph*, October 29, 2004.

4. Comment by J.D., "The Year 2004: Birth (Jonathan Glazer)," *Film for the Soul*, (July 24, 2004), filmforthesoul.blogspot.com/2009/07.

5. "The doctrine of reincarnation is exceedingly unpalatable to many people because it makes each one of us directly responsible for his present condition. We all dislike having to face this responsibility, and some of us prefer to blame God, or our parents, or the existing political system for making us what we are. If we deny reincarnation and claim that this birth is our first, we are, in fact, disclaiming responsibility for our condition; since it then logically follows that this condition must have been ordained by God, or brought about by the influences of heredity and environment. Hence, if we have been born physically or economically underprivileged, we are provided with a permanent grievance, which permits us to spend a lifetime of sulking and cursing our fate, and with a permanent excuse for all our own weaknesses and failures" (*How to Know God, The Yoga Aphorisms of Patanjali*, commentary Swami Prabhavananda and Christopher Isherwood [Hollywood, CA: Vedanta Press, 1981], 118–19).

   Then again, perhaps one *should* feel uncomfortable with the doctrine. Read on: "I know myself as I am; as I appeared or will appear is not within my experience. It is not that I do not remember. In fact there is nothing to remember. Reincarnation implies a reincarnating self. There is no such thing. The bundle of memories and hopes, called the 'I' imagines itself existing everlastingly and creates time to accommodate its false eternity: To *be*, I need no past or future. All experience is born of imagination; I do not imagine, so no birth or death happens to me. Only those who think themselves born can think themselves reborn. . . . All exists in awareness and awareness neither dies or is reborn. It is the changeless reality itself" (Sri Nisargadatta Maharaj, *I Am That*, 262 [see chap. 7, epigraph]).

6. Robert Cumbow, "Why Is This Film Called Birth?: Investigating Jonathan Glazer's Mystery of the Heart," http://www.slantmagazine.com/house/author/rcumbow/.

CHAPTER SIXTEEN

Epigraph. Segal, *Life After Death*, 715 (see introduction, n. 3).

1. Alan F. Segal points out studies showing that in a situation of trauma people close to death may reach a physiological state of disinhibition, a brain malfunction that occurs when nerve fibers fire erratically and stop sending meaningful signals to the central nervous system. These people may experience the long dark tunnel, the bright white light at the end, and the feeling that they are floating toward the light—neurologically determined experiences that feel like being out of the body. "If there is a biological basis for these experiences, there surely is also a broad vocabulary of images which the individual mind brings into the experience, based on personal history, training, and culture. I suggest that the difference between . . . disinhibition and a detailed mystical ascent to heaven is the long mystical training of the adepts who learn both techniques for achieving the physical states and the culture's social and cultural lore about what the state means" (Segal, *Life after Death*, 335–36).
2. Ibid., 713.
3. "Hereafter Movie Review, Pictures—Rotten Tomatoes," http:www. rottentomatoes.com/m/hereafter/.
4. Carol Zaleski, *Otherworld Journeys: Accounts of Near-Death Experience in Medieval and Modern Times* (New York: Oxford University Press, 1987), 205.

CHAPTER SEVENTEEN

Epigraph. Herman Hupfeld, music and lyrics, "As Time Goes By" (Warner Bros. Music Corporation, 1931).

1. The 2008 PBS documentary *Cinema's Exiles: From Hitler to Hollywood* (directed, produced, and written by Karen Thomas) traces the experience of more than three hundred Jews who fled Nazi Germany between 1933

and 1939 and took refuge in Hollywood, examining their impact on German and American cinema.

2. Conrad Veidt was made immortal with his role as Cesare, the somnambulist in Robert Wiene's classic German silent film *Das Kabinet des Dr. Caligari* (1919). David Thomson writes that the character "was a creature from Poe's nightmares, tall, gaunt, glowing with a mixture of illness and ecstatic anxiety . . . an attenuated, hypersensitive figure, the aesthete or artist tormented by dark forces and driven to violence" (*The New Biographical Dictionary of Film* [New York: Alfred A. Knopf, 2004], 917).

CHAPTER EIGHTEEN

Epigraph. T. S. Eliot, "Little Gidding," *Four Quartets* (New York: Harcourt, Brace & World, 1971), 59.

1. One of today's most popular rankings of motion pictures is the Internet Movie Data Base, IMDb (www.imdb.com/). It currently lists the one hundred most popular films, in order, starting with *The Shawshank Redemption* (1994), *The Godfather* (1972), *The Godfather II* (1974), *Pulp Fiction* (1994), and *The Good, the Bad and the Ugly* (1966). *Citizen Kane* (1941) now ranks number forty-six.
2. For more information on the functional dynamics of the instincts, see *The Divine Ideas: The Symbol*, 1st ed., Arica Institute Inc., http://www.arica.org/.

CHAPTER NINETEEN

Epigraph: John C. Eccles, *Evolution of the Brain, Creation of the Self* (Abingdon, Oxon, England: Routledge, 1989), 241.

1. Dante Alighieri, *The Divine Comedy*, Carlyle-Wicksteed trans. (New York: Modern Library, 1950), 11.
2. Wilber, *Up from Eden*, 59 (see chap. 9, epigraph note).

3. His Holiness the Dalai Lama, *Dzogchen: The Heart Essence of the Great Perfection* (Ithaca, NY: Snow Lion Publications, 2001), 99.

4. "Heart Sutra," *Wikipedia*, last modified January 14, 2013, http://en.wikipedia. org/wiki/Heart_Sutra. See also Jan Nattier, "The Heart Sutra: A Chinese Apocryphal Text?," *Journal of the International Association of Buddhist Studies* 15, no. 2 (19920): 153–223.

5. Bhagwan Shree Rajneesh, from *Never Born Never Died*, found on Wikiquote, "Bhagwan Shree Rajneesh," http:// http://en.wikiquote.org/wiki/Osho.

6. *The Kabir Book: Forty-Four of the Ecstatic Poems of Kabir*, versions by Robert Bly (Boston: Beacon Press, 1977), 24–25.

FILMOGRAPHY

A Christmas Carol, 1951, Brian Desmond-Hurst

All of Me, 1984, Carl Reiner

Always, 1989, Steven Spielberg

Angel on My Shoulder, 1946, Archie Mayo

Audrey Rose, 1977, Robert Wise

Between Two Worlds, 1944, Edward A. Blatt

Beetlejuice, 1988, Tim Burton

Beyond Tomorrow, 1939, A. Edward Sutherland

Birth, 2004, Jonathan Glazer

Blithe Spirit, 1945, David Lean

Bruce Almighty, 2003, Tom Shadyac

Cabin in the Sky, 1943, Vincente Minelli

The Canterville Ghost, 1944, Jules Dassin

Casablanca, 1942, Michael Curtiz

Carnival of Souls, 1962, Herk Harvey

Dead of Night, 1945, Cavalcanti, Crichton, Dearden, Hamer

Death Takes A Holiday, 1934, Mitchell Leisen

Defending Your Life, 1991, Albert Brooks

The Devil and Daniel Webster, 1941, William Dieterle

Field of Dreams, 1989, Phil Alden Robinson

Flatliners, 1990, Joel Schumacher

Ghost, 1990, Jerry Zucker

The Ghost and Mrs. Muir, 1947, Joseph Mankiewicz

The Ghost Goes West, 1935, René Clair

Groundhog Day, 1993, Harold Ramis
A Guy Named Joe, 1943, Victor Fleming
Heart and Souls, 1993, Ron Underwood
Heaven Can Wait, 1978, Warren Beatty
Hereafter, 2010, Clint Eastwood
Here Comes Mr. Jordan, 1941, Alexander Hall
Heaven Only Knows, 1947, Arthur S. Rogell
The Horn Blows at Midnight, 1945, Raoul Walsh
The I Inside, 2004, Roland Suso Richter
I Married a Witch, 1942, René Claire
Interview With the Vampire: The Vampire Chronicles, 1994, Neil Jordan
It's a Wonderful Life, 1946, Frank Capra
Jacob's Ladder, 1990, Adrian Lyne
Just Like Heaven, 2005, Mark Waters
Kiss Me Goodbye, 1982, Robert Mulligan
Kundun, 1997, Martin Scorsese
Little Buddha, 1993, Bernardo Bertolucci
Lulu on the Bridge, 1998, Paul Auster
Made In Heaven, 1987, Alan Rudolph
A Matter of Life and Death (*Stairway to Heaven*), 1946, Michael
  Powell/Emeric Pressburger
The Meaning of Life, 1983, Terry Gilliam, Terry Jones
The Other, 1972, Robert Mulligan
The Others, 2001, Alejandro Amenábar
Outward Bound, 1930, Robert Milton
Passengers, 2008, Rodrigo García
Peter Ibbetson, 1935, Henry Hathaway
Poltergeist, 1982, Tobe Hooper
Portrait of Jennie, 1948, William Dieterle
Purgatory, 1999, Uli Edel
The Reincarnation of Peter Proud, 1975, J. Lee Thompson

Resurrection, 1980, Daniel Petrie

The Return of Peter Grimm, (1935), George Nichols, Jr.

The Sixth Sense, 1999, M. Night Shyamalan

Thunder Rock, 1942, Ray Boulting

Topper, 1937, Norman Z. McLeod

Tree of Life, 2011, Terrence Malick

Truly, Madly, Deeply, 1991, Anthony Minghella

The Uninvited, 1944, Lewis Allen

What Dreams May Come, 1998, Vincent Ward

The Wizard of Oz, 1939, Victor Fleming

RESOURCES

For more information about the listed films we recommend:

    Wikipedia: en.wikipedia.org/wiki/Films

    The Internet Movie Database: www.imdb.com

For information and history about the film-blanc genre and the

    motion pictures associated with it, visit www.filmblanc.info/,

    a real treasure trove.

INDEX

INDEX

INDEX

INDEX

Quest Books

encourages open-minded inquiry into
world religions, philosophy, science, and the arts
in order to understand the wisdom of the ages,
respect the unity of all life, and help people explore
individual spiritual self-transformation.

Its publications are generously supported by
The Kern Foundation,
a trust committed to Theosophical education.

Quest Books is the imprint of
the Theosophical Publishing House,
a division of the Theosophical Society in America.
For information about programs, literature,
on-line study, membership benefits, and international centers,
see www.theosophical.org
or call 800-669-1571 or (outside the U.S.) 630-668-1571.

To order books or a complete Quest catalog,
call 800-669-9425 or (outside the U.S.) 630-665-0130.

ABOUT THE AUTHORS

Tom Davis Genelli, PhD, worked as TV-network ABC's film-collection librarian, and later as an independent film producer/director and an instructor in film production at New York's New School for Social Research. After returning to San Francisco for a doctorate in psychology, he served for twenty-six years as the clinical supervisor for Conard House, a large, progressive mental health agency.

Lyn Davis Genelli, MFT, has been a psychotherapist, consultant, and workshop leader for over forty years. She is the cofounder of the Bay Area Institute for Integrative Body Psychotherapy. She also teaches hatha yoga and yoga nidra and is a long-time practitioner of meditation.

The Genellis share a profound conviction that the purpose of life is self-realization for the benefit of all. In the course of their respective careers, they began writing to address the cross-fertilization of film, psychology, and spirituality as a way of expressing this conviction. Their articles have appeared in journals of psychology and popular culture, including *Yoga Journal* and *Vogue*. For more information, see www.deathatthemovies.com.

More Praise for Lyn and Tom Davis Genelli's
Death at the Movies

"With insight and compassion, the Genellis examine classic films to teach us how our personal values shape the transition from life to what comes next. We learn what to expect when we let go of what is familiar and safe and head into the unknown."

—Tom Ruffles, author of *Ghost Images: Cinema of the Afterlife*

"An important work existing on many levels—spiritual, cultural, philosophical—and a book that deserves to be read. It contains lucid and profound insights that resonate deeply with a classic choice of films, as well as, of course, with life itself."

—Rudy Wurlitzer, screen writer and author

"This amazing book informs while it entertains, weaving classic cinema with the soul's journey. It captures the essence of a highly charged subject with respect and humor. A delicious read!"

—Everett Aison, artist and Founder/Director of the New York School of Visual Arts